Marilyn — with my very best wishes
Ken

PUTTING MONEY IN ITS PLACE

---

by Ken Rouse

Center for the Study of
Religion and Society
4020 Nanovic Hall
Notre Dame, IN 46556

THE ROUSE COMPANIES • PHOENIX, ARIZONA

Dedication

Dedicated to those who search for direction in the use of their money and to the emerging profession of financial advisors—in the hope that this book will help them listen and respond effectively to one another.

Acknowledgments

While the idea for this book was my own and is an integral part of my mission in life, there are many people who helped make it happen. Friends, family and clients encouraged me and offered appreciated support for the completion of the book.

As an experienced editor, Fran Fielding-Jones skillfully coordinated the completion of my writing efforts. I was impressed with her ability to preserve my concepts and style of expression while contributing significantly to the translation of the message for the reader.

While it is difficult to put this thought and feeling into words, I must acknowledge that Higher Purpose which gives meaning to this and every project I've undertaken in my life. Beyond all of our collective efforts and understanding, there is a destiny that makes the process worthwhile.

Contents

Welcome to a discussion of money
which does not begin with money at all.

It starts with *you!*

Mark is a 38-year-old engineer, earning over $50,000 a year, who has acquired a few impressive investments over the last 10 years. He works hard and dreams of making $100,000 and doubling the value of his investments in the next three years. Ask him "why?", and he will answer "I don't know. Don't you think that's a good idea?"

Joan and Randy are a dual-income professional couple, and their combined earnings are well into the six figures. Although they have such a comfortable income, they have saved little. Other than the company benefit programs, they have no investments and aren't sure where their money goes. If you asked them "Are you having fun yet," they would look at each other and shrug their shoulders as if to indicate they hadn't thought much about it.

CHAPTER 1

You Are More Important Than Your Money

Welcome to a discussion of money which does not begin with money at all. It starts with *you!*

What is most important to you? What makes you feel good?

What are your current goals for this time of your life?

What would you like to do in the years ahead?

Do you want to enjoy today while making sure you have a secure tomorrow? If so, how do you achieve that balance?

Just having *more* money is not the answer. Having *enough* money, however, is essential, and the critical question is "How much is enough for you?" Money's prime function is a simple one: to help you achieve what you desire most in your life.

How to put *you* before money is a subject as vital as any you will ever address. In fact, since our financial decisions reflect our personal values, having a better perspective about money may result in many other areas of your life falling into place.

Having perspective about money is vital. In fact, more sensitive than sex, more powerful than politics, is the intimate subject of money in your life.

A recent survey, for example, showed that people think more

about money than about sex. Yet many people have found that talking about money is even more intimate, more awkward than discussing sex or other personal matters. Perhaps this is true because it forces them to reveal aloud what they really value deep down inside. Moreover, explaining to someone else why you spend money as you do also can reveal some of your dreams, aspirations, and basic personality. This is highly personal territory.

Yet the choice of where to put our money *should* be one which flows naturally from being in touch with what is truly important to us. That means knowing now what we value most, and staying in touch with our feelings now—and as they change in the years ahead.

It means communicating clearly with other significant people in our lives and with anyone who is involved as an advisor to us. The better we understand ourselves and what life means to us, the easier it is to keep money in perspective. Taking charge of our lives enables us to control what we do with our money.

Many of us have enjoyed going through the "fun house" at amusement parks or fairs where special mirrors distort our image. We can see ourselves looking taller, shorter, heavier, thinner. We find it amusing to see how we would look if we could change our bodies. Suppose, however, that we could find a mirror that would show us now how we would look ten, twenty or thirty years from now. There would be obvious physical changes: graying, perhaps, or more face lines, or a changed figure for some. But what else would you see as you look closely at the you that is to be? Are you smiling contentedly or looking bitter? Do you look prosperous or shabby? Are you standing tall and proud of what you've accomplished, or embarrassed and uncertain? Do you like what you see?

More important, in looking at the future, do you want to do something today to make sure that the person you will be thirty years from now is the one you want to be? That's what financial planning is all about: seeing where you are and where you want to be, and taking action to bring about the results you desire.

16

The focus of this book, then, is on helping you develop a financial plan which is best suited for your own individual, personal needs. It will help you take inventory of where you are today, set realistically achievable goals for the future, and then identify specifically the steps you need to take in order to achieve those goals. *Your* goals. After all, it is your life and your money.

Know Thyself

We all know about Shakespeare's advice "to thine ownself be true" and the counsel to "know thyself" which is inscribed at the Delphic Oracle, which symbolized wisdom in the ancient Greek civilization.

In the financial planning process, that means trying to understand what money means to you, why you spend and why you save, what you buy and what you forego, why you take risks or are afraid to, what kind of lifestyle you have now and what you want in the future.

Money can be one of the most powerful ingredients in making your lifestyle dreams come true. You begin to understand the power of money, however, only when you think about it in terms that are very personal, very specific and very practical. In other words, when you think about *your* money, ask yourself how you feel about the way you are using it today to enjoy life—and what you are doing with it to secure tomorrow?

The words "personal," "specific," and "practical" are key words.

We are not all alike. We don't have the same needs, we don't have the same amount of money, we are not in the same tax brackets, we are not willing to take the same risks, and we don't even want the same results from the use of our money. So there has to be a way for you to ask and answer questions that are designed to help you get what *you* want and need out of the management of your money.

17

To begin with, let's take a look at some of the questions we should be asking.

First of all, you have to know what you *want*: that means clarifying your own personal values and setting definite and realistic goals.

Second, you need to know what you *have*: that means taking inventory of your financial resources.

Third, you have to look at and evaluate the various alternatives for reaching your goals, based on what you *want* and on what you *have*.

Sociologist Abraham Maslow's study of human motivation identified the needs most people were seeking to satisfy. In ascending order, his Hierarchy of Needs listed:

1) Physiological needs, such as food and clothing

2) Safety and stability

3) Belonging and love

4) Esteem

5) Self-actualization

What we discover, of course, in real life situations is that this is highly subjective. People do not take care of their needs necessarily in the order of the hierarchy. It's not unusual to see people spend money to satisfy personal esteem even if they have to do without something as basic as food. What the hierarchy does, however, is to help us recognize perhaps more clearly that there are trade-offs.

Understanding who we are, what we need, and what we want greatly improves planning; but we also need to recognize that it will never be perfect. We will probably spend the rest of our lives planning for many things that never happen and we will also, in the future, be dealing with many things we did not plan for. It is obvious, therefore, that we must also plan for flexibility.

Making Dreams Come True

Most people certainly dream of one day being financially independent. Although, to some, the term "financial independence" may sound abstract and distant, it is nevertheless a desired goal for the future. Once you get involved, however, in the process of planning for financial independence, you discover that it is not a static, rocking-chair state at all. It is dynamic and energizing. In fact, financial independence creates the kind of freedom which opens doors to possibilities for living which we might not have even dreamed were possible.

You see, when you are truly financially set, you no longer have to work. You are not dependent upon your own labor or service to make a living. You can actually choose to do whatever you want to do with your life. That's exciting!

It is incredible how many people go through life saying, "I can't do this or I can't do that because I have to work. My 'job' comes first." Well, financial independence enables us to quit playing that self-defeating game. With financial independence, if we truly want to spend our time and energy working at our job, we are free to do that. It doesn't become a "have to." We can be honest and say that that's what we want to do. Think of the new results that are possible from your job when you are able to make that kind of honest commitment to it. On the other hand, if there are creative "non-income producing activities" to which we would like to give our time and attention, financial independence literally makes that choice possible.

Putting Wings On Our Dreams

Some people have indicated that they would like to achieve financial independence very early in life. Most people would like at least to get there by the time they reach age 65. Unfortunately, the vast majority of people do not achieve that goal at all.

Research and studies continue to reveal that a large percentage of the people who reach age 65 are still financially dependent. They are either dependent upon family or government or charity, or else they are forced to work to make the money required to live. It has been said that people do not *plan* to *fail*. Most people, however, do *fail* to *plan*. The result is that their dream of financial independence may not come true.

Yet all of us have, at one time or another, not only dreamed about being financially independent, but have also fantasized about finding a magic answer to all of our financial problems. If you could just win that big lottery, or if someone would come along and show you how to get rich with no money to begin with and little effort on your part! Well, as you know, that's not the way it works for most people.

Yet dreams for the future are a very important part of living. All of us at times think about the future and what we would like it to be. For some, those dreams may be fuzzy and undefined, but nevertheless the dreams are there. Some of our dreams may be realistic and some may be extremely colorful and exciting, perhaps unachievable, perhaps not.

Some of us even get around to developing plans to make some of those dreams come true. There are very few dreams, however, that materialize without a plan. Maybe, in fact, that explains why so few dreams come true—because so few people actually plan. Planning, with our feet on the ground, puts wings on our dreams.

About 2,000 years ago, the Roman philosopher Seneca wrote: "Our plans miscarry because we have no aim. When a man does not know what harbor he is making for, no wind is the right wind."

Your Own Perspective

To start with, you need to look at where you are now in developing a personal plan. Maybe you're already off and running. That's great! But have you asked yourself if you're running in the direction you really want to go? Or maybe, like many people, you're too busy to plan or are having difficulty getting started.

In developing a plan, there is, as you undoubtedly realize, no "one way" for everyone. If we were to take a thousand people, there would be the potential for at least a thousand different plans. So, how do you go about finding the plan that is right for you? How do you sort through all the confusing alternatives and conflicting advice? How do you avoid the paralysis of analyzing one situation after another without acting on any of them? How do you make decisions and take the action you need to take in the financial arena of your life?

It does not greatly matter what other people are doing. In fact, it is said that if you want to act creatively and responsibly, look at what everybody else is doing—and then don't do it. While this may have been uttered tongue-in-cheek, it is essential to have your own perspectives based on the way you view life.

Suppose that there are 20 people in a locked room; 19 have been brainwashed to believe they were having a party. One person has not been brainwashed. What you can see as you look into the room is 19 people having a good time and one person frantically trying to get the others to help break down the door. It appears, does it not, that the one person is mad and the others are having a good time. Then, suddenly, you are allowed to see what the one person is seeing through a window. You can see a tidal wave coming toward the 20 people in the locked room.

It is now obvious that the only person in the room who sees the tidal wave is the one who has not been brainwashed. Suddenly, you change your mind and decide the 19 are mad and the one is sane. Your mind has changed because your knowledge and perception have changed.

In the financial planning process, as in all areas of life, it is essential to question the standards set by others and to continue adding knowledge and clear perspectives on what you want out of life.

As you gain greater knowledge of yourself and of what you expect, the more confidence you will gain and the more tuned in you will be to articulating what is really important to you—and how to use money to achieve it.

The Real Questions

Reflect for a minute on what is probably happening right now in your own life situation.

You listen to other people, right? They tell you what they think you ought to do. Why, then, don't you do it? Probably because you realize that they are limited in their own experience and can't really know what is best for you.

You are trying to decide what to do with some of your money. You listen to an advertisement that says, "put your money here, invest with us." You hear the experts boast that, "when they talk, people listen." Somehow, you are not convinced! There are times when you are almost persuaded, and you have made a few stabs in the dark. For the most part, however, you are still confused by conflicting advice, too many alternatives, and a basic lack of confidence in your own planning direction.

Maybe it would be different if you had lots of money, but you have to be careful with your funds and make sure that you get the results you want from the management and use of your money. The results are, in fact, directly related to how well you ask and answer the real questions of your life.

The real questions are not general. They are not questions such as "where is a good place to put money?" or, "how do you avoid paying taxes?" Anyone who is quick to answer these general questions for you cannot possibly know if your best interest is being served. The real questions are personal, specific, and practical.

In Itself, Money Has No Value

An important point to remember is that the most meaningful discussions about money do not actually begin with money itself.

Why is that? Well, because money, in and of itself, has no real value. We talk about what inflation does to the value of money. However, what we are referring to is the purchasing power of the dollar. Fifteen years ago the purchasing power of a dollar was about twice as much as it is today. In other words, it takes about $2.00 today to purchase what $1.00 would have bought fifteen years ago. The impact of inflation over the last 30 years has probably raised the cost of living to the point where it requires almost $4.00 today to purchase what $1.00 would have bought 30 years ago.

Another example: in 1914, Henry Ford paid his workers $5.00 a day and, with that high wage (for 1914), Henry Ford created a middle class.

Since money itself has no inherent value, as we indicated, it is one's purchasing power, rather than the number of dollars one has, that matters.

Nevertheless, money is tremendously important! It is essential in the business of living because it is the way we purchase what we decide has value to us. If, one day, we go back to the barter system, and money is no longer important, we can change the whole process. As long as money is the method by which we put a price tag on our values, however, we have to understand how money and our values go together.

Let me give you an example which dramatically illustrates the fact that money, in and of itself, has no value. Some years ago, a woman was invited into the trust department of a bank and told about her inheritance. She was ecstatic! In fact, she was so excited about what had happened that she rushed out into the street and told nearby strangers how rich she was. How much money had she inherited? A little less than $25,000.

Shortly thereafter, another woman was also invited into the trust department of the bank and told about an awaited inheritance. She was depressed. She burst into tears. She was desperate; she didn't know if she could go on. How was she going to continue to live in the manner to which she had become accustomed? Was there going to be enough income from her inheritance to take care of the maids, gardeners, chauffeurs, to pay for her extensive travel and the lavish parties which she had always provided for a multitude of friends? What was her inheritance? Five million in cash.

Obviously then, money, in and of itself, is important only as it helps us obtain what we really need and want and what is wanted and needed differs dramatically for all of us.

The Price Of Pleasure

Consider the most important activities in your preferred lifestyle. What are you doing when you are doing what you really want to do? What turns you on? What activities give you the greatest pleasure? It helps to be as specific as possible. Make an educated guess as to the cost of those activities in today's dollars. You can estimate the cost on a monthly or an annual basis.

This exercise usually surprises most people. Some discover that the price tag attached to what they enjoy most is considerably greater than they imagined, while others are surprised at how little it costs for them to do what matters most in life. I'm convinced that the millions of Americans who enjoy jogging didn't choose to run only because it was cheaper than yachting.

Oscar Wilde once defined a cynic as a man who knows the price of everything, and the value of nothing.

What is important to most of us is to calculate the price of things only after we know what we truly value. That critical first step will enable us to proceed with putting our money in its place, and then it is much more likely that we will succeed in finding the right places to put our money.

Your Personal Action Plan

Before you go on to the next chapter, take a few minutes to reflect on what you have read. Consider the Action Item on the next page as a catalyst to get you started writing down what you need to Act-On in order to benefit personally from the time you have invested reading this far.

At the end of each chapter you will have an opportunity to take time out for an ACT-I-ON.

ACT·I·ON

1. I will spend some quality time (an hour or more) identifying why I am more important than my money.

2. I will start making a list of ways in which I can be in charge of my life and get my money to work for me.

When Lori, a young unmarried market researcher earning a $30,000 salary, sat down one day to look at her spending plan, it was almost unbelievable to her how much she was spending on items which she didn't particularly care about. Although she herself was not a skiing enthusiast, she had purchased expensive ski clothes and equipment and gone along on frequent skiing weekends just to be with her friends. Not once had she stepped back to ask how she really felt about the way she was spending her money.

In their early 50's, Glenn and Arlene now have a complicated investment portfolio, consisting of stocks inherited from their parents, "deals" recommended by Glenn's fellow executives at the hotel he manages, and several programs which they are now discussing with their not-so-friendly district representative from the Internal Revenue Service. Their financial decisions have usually been made on the spur of the moment in response to suggestions or what was being heavily advertised.

CHAPTER 2

Planning From The Inside-Out

Working Backwards

We usually talk about money in terms of economic conditions, tax reform, interest rates, stock quotations, and real estate values. We ask people for investment tips, or we grab the newspaper each morning to check how certain investments have performed so we can determine whether to buy or sell.

There's a basic problem in developing a financial plan by concentrating on investment markets, however; it traps you into an approach that we call planning from the outside-in.

It's an approach which ignores some of the essential ingredients which should be considered when investing. It ignores you and your life. It doesn't take into account, for example:

- who you are
- how you feel
- how much you have to invest
- what risks you are willing to take
- and the results you expect.

Planning From The Inside-Out

A much more sensible approach to developing a life-long successful financial plan starts not with either money markets or even money itself.

Start instead with yourself . . . with what makes you unique and special . . . with what you value in your life.

That's what we call planning from the inside-out.

Asking "Why?"

There is no long-range financial plan or life plan which can be effective which does not begin with our own "soul searching" and effort to plan from the inside-out.

"Planning from the inside-out" means asking the "why" questions as well as the "what" questions. Not only must we ask what we want to accomplish, but why it is important to us, and how we expect to feel when we have achieved the goals we've set.

Why is it important to have money for the future? Or why is it important to take more time for the enjoyment of the present? Why is it important to some of us to take the risk of succeeding in something which is uncertain instead of settling for the security of a job with a more certain future? Or why is it more important for others to have a fixed or somewhat guaranteed income versus the risk associated with an opportunity for unusual gain?

Once we have dealt with the "whys" of life, we are then prepared to deal with what must be done to accomplish our objectives. By asking the "how" questions, we begin to bridge the gap between the inside and outside. "How will I get this job done? How will I get from here to there?"

The answers to these questions depend on ourselves as much as they do on any financial resources available for our consideration. In fact, they may help us understand better what our financial resources really are.

How Can I Manage Money Which I Don't Have?

One of the most frequent questions we get from participants in our

30

seminar/workshops is, "How can I manage money which I don't have?" The essence of that question is that there seems to be nothing left over after the salary or earnings have been spent, and to date it has not been possible to accumulate any savings or investments to worry about. The fallacy, of course, in this thinking is that it supposes a situation in which the individuals are victims.

They seem to feel the world has dealt them a bad hand, and they have no choice in the matter.

If more money coming in is part of the solution, there are ways for us to increase our earnings. We don't have to become workaholics in order to do that. Sometimes, right in front of our eyes there is a fun project or hobby which can be translated into a money-making activity. For example, someone with artistic or crafts ability can develop a meaningful second income and enjoy that activity on evenings and weekends. However, even if your only source of earnings is your basic job itself, you can employ the approach of balancing expenditures for today's enjoyment with the allocation of funds for tomorrow's enjoyment. This is a balance *you* can create.

It is amazing to see how many people go through life telling themselves there is no money left for savings, without realizing that the situation exists because of their own decisions.

We have worked with many clients whose incomes were as much as several hundred thousand dollars a year. Many of them were complaining that they did not have enough money at the end of the month and could not possibly save. That is a mind-set which results in our doing something to ourselves. It is not something which the world has done to us.

There are many people who may echo the words of Howard, a 45-year-old architect, who earns $75,000 a year, is divorced, and lives with his teen-age son. "I believe that most people who like things tend to keep them," says Howard. "If that's true, it must be that I really don't like money, because I don't keep it very long. It just seems to slip through my fingers."

31

A story is told of a conversation among a member of the clergy, a physician and a psychologist. It seems that they were discussing the question, "When does life begin?" The clergyman said that life begins with conception. The physician, on the other hand, felt that life begins when the child is born. After thoughtful reflection, the psychologist suggested that perhaps life begins when the children move away.

Regardless of how we define "life," when we can integrate our financial planning with our life planning, we add a new dimension to living.

Whether your income is $30,000 or $300,000 per year, it is the allocation of those dollars which brings your lifestyle into focus. We cannot separate the dollars required from the values to which we are committed.

The basic objective of the planning process is, therefore, essentially the same for everyone.

It is to utilize your resources: (1) to create a lifestyle which reflects your values for the present and the future, and (2) to coordinate the making of money and the management of money to achieve the results you desire throughout your lifetime.

Making money is not a goal in itself. *Managing* money is not the goal. Making and managing money are simply means to an end, and we define that end by going back to our personal life values and determining what is important. Once that has been done, we have a personalized blueprint for implementing a financial plan that will work best.

Getting In Touch With Yourself

It seems, however, that getting in touch with our innermost feelings is a difficult challenge for most people.

For example: Nicholas was an enthusiastic psychology major in college. Today, he is a businessman with a career in the field of manufacturing, but he still continues to read about and pursue the new developments in the field of psychology. He is now ready to get serious about being self-directed in his financial planning. What happens? His habits of studying and analyzing other people's thoughts and behavior prevail. He spends almost two years exploring all the various schools of thought on how money can be and is often used by people to exercise their emotions of fear and greed. He even takes on a project to put together 101 ways in which money can be used to manipulate.

Nowhere in the process, however, does Nicholas get in touch with his own internal thoughts and feelings about what he really wants out of life and how he can use his own financial resources to achieve his goal. His external research is actually a subtle distraction from the primary objective. He is again looking outside himself for answers.

Asking "Why?"

Most people have similar difficulties in focusing inward. Getting in touch with our innermost feelings, admittedly, is not an easy process. While we focus on how we feel about things at this point in time, we have to recognize that we are, in many ways, a product of many external influences which began at birth.

Did we come from a rich, poor, or middle-class environment? What were our parents' attitudes toward money? How deeply ingrained are their attitudes in us? Did we adopt their attitudes or, for many personal reasons, determine to live with a completely opposite point of view? Did our mother and father have differing approaches to saving and spending? What effect did that have on us?

Even outside the home, we may have been influenced by schoolmates and friends. Later on, by the kind of jobs we had and, certainly, by the attitudes of those with whom we fell in love.

Our lives undoubtedly will continue to be shaped by influences of all kinds from the world in which we live. The objective is not to dismiss external influences from our lives, but to put them in perspective.

You might try doing the following exercise with someone you're close to. However, you can also wear two hats and try it alone. The idea is to probe into some basic attitudes until you have found your true feelings underneath the surface.

Begin by making a statement such as, "The way I feel about money is . . ." and then finish the statement. When you have done so, then the question is why? Why do you feel that way? Pursue the feelings further by continuing, "The reason I feel that way is because . . ." When you have finished verbalizing those feelings, press again with the question, "Why do you feel that way?"

Regardless of whether someone else is helping with the questioning or whether you are your own interrogator, you will undoubtedly experience some impatience with the process. The natural response after a few attempts is to say, "Well, I already told you why." Rather than stop short, however, with one or two answers, push yourself until you have probed more deeply each time with stronger feelings and deeper insight into the "why" of your previous answer. You will be surprised at the discoveries you will make if you stay with the process.

Let me give you an example. Walter is a 27-year-old paint company salesman who had turned down an opportunity to transfer to another region as an assistant sales manager. In response to the first "why" as to the reason for refusing the transfer, Walter began the questioning process several years ago by saying, "I don't feel that money is important." Then, there was the question, why? To which he replied, "Because it seems to get in the way and often does more harm than it does good." Again, why? Walter hesitated and when he continued, he himself seemed surprised at his answer. "Because," he said, "I just realized that money is what seemed to take all of my father's time. I guess I resented that he cared more for making money than he did for me. I never really did get to know him because he was constantly pursuing more and more money.

34

"Also," Walter admitted, "it was my wife's obsession with money that led finally to our divorce."

Again, there was the question, "Why? Why do you feel that way?" "Because that is exactly what happened," Walter snapped. Gently, the question came again. "And why do you feel that that's exactly what happened?" Walter thought about it. "Maybe it wasn't really what made my father or wife act the way they did," he said. "Actually, I really don't know what was important to either my father or my ex-wife. In fact, I probably never got to know either of them well enough." And why? "Because I was too busy assuming how they felt and reacting to the way *I* thought they felt about money." And why? Walter almost whispered, "I guess I really don't know, but I do know that's where I need to start."

Walter became aware that he had always been afraid to let money become important. He had been reacting emotionally to what seemed to be the loss of people close to him and looking for a reason outside the personal relationship. While there was no overnight magic in the questioning process, it did enable Walter to gain new perspective on the meaning of money in his own life. He realized that, deep down, money *was* important to him. By trying to ignore its importance, money was exercising an amazing amount of control over the way he lived. By putting his real attitude toward money in perspective, however, he was able to set priorities on the things he truly valued and reconsider his career goals.

When Financial Attitudes Differ

Before you make important financial decisions, it is essential not only to know why and what you want, but also why and what the people want who are involved in your life.

A few years after she was divorced, Virginia met and married Joe and brought her teen-age daughter, Kelly, to live with them.

Both Joe and Virginia are employed and, in fact, they earn about the same amount of money which they contribute to their family income. The control of the money, however, is in Joe's hands.

Joe boasts about being frugal. He is a saver. He doesn't feel comfortable spending much money, and so, most of what Joe and Virginia earn is salted away in safe, conservative accounts.

Virginia, on the other hand, believes in having a good time and doesn't feel that she is getting much from her hard work and growing income. There are increasing conflicts over the subject of money. Virginia often feels tired after a day's work and would like to go out for dinner. She says she needs good clothes for herself at the office and for Kelly to keep up with her friends at school. She wants to give Kelly a car as a high school graduation gift and, if Kelly wants to go to college, pay for her daughter's tuition at a good school. Joe is fighting her all the way on what he considers an extravagant lifestyle.

The turnaround for Joe and Virginia was a session with a qualified counselor and financial advisor who did not rush to the solution, but instead, took time to listen and help Joe and Virginia define the problem. They were both given an opportunity to express how they felt about money and were asked the "why" questions.

It turned out that Joe grew up during the depression. His father worked hard to earn the family money (what little there was). His mother did an amazing job of managing what little his father made and even saving some money in the process. Even though Joe was now making a six-figure salary and Virginia was bringing in about an equal amount, he was still operating on the emotions that he learned as a child.

On the other hand, Virginia—who also grew up in a very difficult financial situation—used to hear her mother fantasize about being rich, being able to travel, and to afford good things.

While in Virginia's home they had very little and spent what they had, there was the constant escape in imagining what money could do to bring joy and pleasure to life.

Over a period of time, as they continued to share their feelings,

Joe and Virginia developed a much deeper understanding of themselves and each other. They began to realize that their different attitudes toward child-rearing were more important than what to spend, or not to spend, on Kelly. Once they came to grips with fundamental issues, they could accommodate each other in practical decision-making regarding eating out, clothing, college and other savings vs. spending areas.

A Balanced Personality

We mentioned that even though Joe was now successful, his background still brought about emotions in him that he had learned as a child.

Several years ago, Transactional Analysis encouraged us to recognize that we have, within ourselves, several different ego states. In healthy terms these are described as 1) Parent (nurturing) 2) Adult (realistic and objective) and 3) Child (natural and expressive).

In a sense, the balance between the parent and child within us is achieved by the adult in us. At our best, we never lose the established values of our nurturing parent. Nor do we lose the impulsive freedom and love of life which our natural child creates. It is the balance between the two which gives us character.

In much the same way, we can compare the balance described earlier of "enjoying today" and "planning for tomorrow." You might look at the nurturing parent inside you as the message center for the need to plan, to save and invest for the security of the future. The natural child within you creates the ability to have fun living each new day as it comes. The objective adult, which is the realistic you, enables you to find the right balance. In the complexity of making decisions regarding your present enjoyment of life and your need for future security, you do not have to give up either one for the other. In fact, that would throw your life out of balance. As an adult, you are able to pull together the facts in your situation, examine honestly your own personal feelings, and make decisions which keep you in realistic balance and on track.

We get our best results when:

- Our value system says "yes," that's right for you. You should do that.

- It's realistic for us to take the chosen course of action.

- We enjoy what we are doing.

Planning For Change

"Planning from the inside-out" also implies a willingness to change if our carefully thought-through plans call for it. Yet the willingness to change is not universal.

When they assess their situations, goals and objectives, most people quickly admit they want things to improve. Some, however, are not sure exactly what they want to change; others feel they don't know how to effect the change they want; and others are simply reluctant to make changes.

As we develop our own plans, it might be interesting to recognize how some people rationalize their lack of action. Here are a few of the more typical excuses.

Adam: "I don't want to think about the future. It makes me anxious and uncertain. How can you plan when there are so many unknowns in the future anyway?"

Barbara: "I may be rescued from having to worry about this. I may win a lottery, marry or inherit wealth."

Carol: "Don't ask me to think about what I want. Just tell me what is available and what you think I should do."

David: "I have a business to run and a family which expects me to be with them. I just don't have time for detailed planning."

Evelyn: "If I stay here and do a good job, the company will take care of my financial security, and I won't need to do any planning on my own."

Frank: "My financial future is controlled by the government and by world economic conditions, not by me. I just hope the right forces are in power."

Gordon: "If I had started when I was younger, maybe planning would have helped. But at my age, it's too late to do any serious planning."

Consistent with these approaches is another tendency: to put off serious financial planning until tomorrow, assuming that it will be easier in the future than it is today. Here, too, there are endless excuses: "We have young dependent children." "We have children to educate." "We have a house to pay for first." Obviously, the world offers us many excuses if we are looking for reasons not to achieve. However, the world also offers us many opportunities when we begin to believe in ourselves and our potential.

It is important to note that, even in the most uncertain times, there have always been individuals who move ahead in successful planning patterns. What distinguishes those who achieve results from those who do not seems to be self-confidence and willingness to act. If we do not expect results, we will not get results.

That is why developing a plan for balanced living should be considered at an early point in our lives. One woman in her late 20's, who attended a seminar several years ago, said she had not yet "gotten around" to making a long-range plan. Patricia was an actuary working for a large insurance company, sharing an apartment—and its costs—with a friend. They loved sailing and, together, they bought a boat which not only used up Patricia's savings in the initial purchase, but was costly to maintain. During the seminar discussions, Patricia admitted that while she still took great pleasure in sailing, the weather in her area of the country was such that they were able to use the boat only infrequently.

When she realized that there were other activities she enjoyed which she wanted to have in the future, she soon sold her interest in the boat to her friend, opened an Individual Retirement Account the next year, and took advantage of the matching savings plan provided by her employer. Now she is actually saving 50% of her salary. On her own initiative, she has developed a plan of spending the first paycheck of each month and saving the second paycheck of the month in order to accumulate funds for investing and for purchasing a summer home in the country. That investment requires a nest-egg with which to begin.

She is enthusiastic about this new planning process and would tell you quickly that she is not depriving herself. In fact, she has everything she really needs *today*, but she also has some exciting expectations about tomorrow. She is confident that she can achieve financial independence before she reaches age 50. That will be a significant accomplishment since she is not receiving an income on the higher end of the scale.

It is never easier to begin planning tomorrow, unless we have found the discipline to begin the process today.

Moreover, if we're not careful, we can wait too long. If we do not take inventory, plan and take appropriate action today, inevitably the day will come when we panic and try to play catch up. We cannot achieve any real financial success if we wait for the world to provide us with the answers.

Instead of asking, "What does the world have to offer?," we might ask instead, "What can *I* do to get the results I want from the world?"

By carefully planning from the inside-out, we begin to find answers that make sense for us.

ACT-I-ON

I will answer these three questions (in writing):

1. *What* do I want to accomplish?

2. *Why* is that important to me?

3. *How* do I expect to feel when I reach my goal?

After Alice went through a bad marriage and a bitter divorce, she was determined to change her lifestyle and enjoy each day fully. She has begun taking golf lessons, is redecorating her home, and starting to do volunteer work in her community.

However, there is a nagging reminder that she has done very little to plan for the future. Although she has funds from the divorce and a small inheritance today, she has no idea what her situation will be when she is 60 years old. She is already 53. She is beginning to panic a little when she looks into the future and can't see very clearly.

CHAPTER 3

Getting Your Life In Balance

The Importance Of Balance

It is interesting to note that the Chinese are still guided by a centuries-old belief that both humans and nature must have a perfect balance of yin and yang ("equal and opposite forces") to function properly.

It is incredible how important balance is in the overall experience of living. From the moment you are born, you are in the process of acquiring the right balance to be able to function as a total, integrated human being. Early on, you start to develop the physical balance to be able to walk. Later, you acquire the mental balance to be able to talk; that means you can understand your own thoughts and feelings well enough to communicate them effectively. And then, finally, you develop the emotional balance to interact as an adult with other human beings. It's the balance between giving and receiving that enables you to experience fulfillment in your own life and contribute to fulfillment in the lives of others.

As we consider how money can help us achieve our short- *and* long-range goals, we are talking about achieving a balance between enjoying today and securing tomorrow.

All of us want to be able, do we not, to enjoy today. We also like that good feeling that comes from knowing that we are doing what we need to do to make tomorrow secure.

Go For? Or Forego?

The problem is that life can get out of balance when we get caught up in the busy-ness of living.

As you look at the "balanced living scales" on page 45, with "enjoy today" on one side and "secure tomorrow" on the other, which way do you find yourself leaning?

Do you feel that in your own life situation right now the scales may be tipped a little in the direction of securing tomorrow? You are spending most of your activity, your energy, your time in trying to put aside everything you can for the future. The days just seem to slip past as you work one day after another. You find it difficult to stop and smell the roses—to really enjoy life today.

On the other hand, perhaps you find yourself tipping the scales on the other side. You do a pretty good job, as a matter of fact, experiencing the moment. You know how to have fun. The problem is that you don't spend much time thinking about the future. When tomorrow comes into your mind, you may even have a tendency to worry and you don't like to worry. So you take a time-capsule and try to get back to having fun right now.

Well-balanced living sacrifices neither today nor tomorrow. We give ourselves permission to really enjoy today because we know we are doing what we need to do about tomorrow.

We have all seen examples of such problems in balancing the various aspects of life. The engineering student who spends all his time on his courses in physics, calculus and computer science, with no time for an evening at the movies or visiting with friends, may have narrowed his focus to the point that he finds his studies unfulfilling—and stops studying altogether. The employee, on the other hand, who spends more time at work socializing than getting the job done may find himself out of a job.

Financially speaking, the impact of an imbalance is the same. It is possible to have more money than we could ever spend, yet have lives that are harried, unhappy, and far from fulfilling. It is also

Balanced Living

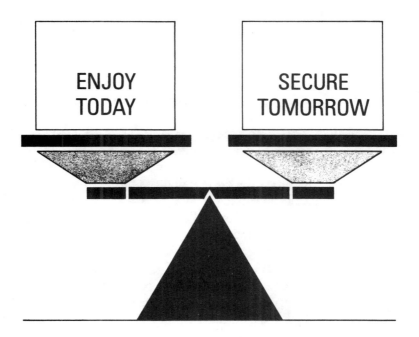

possible to be in control in every way except financially, only to find that our financial problems affect our physical, mental, and emotional health. We have seen physical superstars, or mental giants, whose lives fell apart when they encountered financial disasters.

Consider two fairly typical examples. Jeff and Brian are both 40 years old. Although their incomes are significantly different, their lifestyles are similar. They may both suffer in the future because they have not found a way to balance spending and saving today.

Jeff earns $45,000 a year and has a modest amount of personal property. He and his wife dress well, have two nice cars, quality household furnishings and a few expensive original paintings, but almost no investment assets. Yet, he continues to talk naively about retiring at age 50, and the retirement lifestyle he hopes for is somewhat extravagant.

Even though Brian makes over $250,000 a year, he pays a sizable amount of his income in taxes and spends most of what is left on consumable items such as a lavish wardrobe, travel, and an expensive sports car which he trades in every year for a new one. Brian feels that it is impossible to ever get ahead and doesn't believe he will ever be able to quit working or even slow down.

In both instances, the missing ingredient is a basic understanding of how to balance the present and the future.

You may recall the comic poet Ogden Nash's lines:

"O money, money, money, I'm not necessarily one of those
who think thee holy,
But I often stop to wonder how thou canst go out so fast when
thou comest in so slowly."

When money goes out faster than it comes in, or if out-go or expenses always equals income, it makes no difference how much you earn. Until you begin to manage what you make, the goal of financial independence will elude you. As long as you are dependent each year upon what you earn to support your way of life, you are short-circuiting your ability to enjoy the freedom afforded by financial independence. The key, of course, is to make sure that you use part of your income each year to create a pool of funds large enough to take care of you in the years ahead. That is what managing money is all about.

Obviously, no one can tell you exactly how to achieve that balance in your life. However, that's what planning does for you. It brings you back again and again to find that balance which is right for you. It helps you define what you're doing with your money so you can experience what you want from your life—both today and tomorrow.

The Impact of Imbalance

When we lose our sense of balance physically, mentally, or emotionally, we either figure out what's wrong and correct it, or the imbalance in one area of our lives may eventually create problems in other areas.

For example, everyone today is aware of the importance of physical fitness. Art is someone who started taking seriously his physical well-being several years ago, began jogging on a daily basis, and soon developed a genuine enthusiasm for the whole concept of physical fitness. At this point, running has become an obsession for Art, not only in a physical sense, but also emotionally. He runs ten miles a day, reads books about running in his spare time, and frequently travels on weekends to participate in marathons in various locations.

He spends less and less time with his family, so that important thoughts and activities are no longer shared. At work, he's distracted and can't wait to leave the office for his evening jogging schedule. Neither his wife nor co-workers feel they can count on him.

Unless he stops long enough to deal realistically with his job, his family and other aspects of his life that he might value, Art's life will not be in balance.

47

More Is Not Better...

"The love of money is the root of all evil."—I Timothy 6:10

"Lack of money is the root of all evil."—George Bernard Shaw

Both of these seemingly conflicting statements are probably true. The essential point is that no matter how much money we aspire to, or how little we earn, no matter how much or how little we have accumulated to date, balance is possible if we understand what money means to us, take inventory, set realistic goals, and commit to appropriate action steps.

Let's begin responding to the challenges of organizing our financial lives with a not-so-obvious observation. *More is not better!* If it were, then the richest people would be the best, the happiest, the most fulfilled. History, however, reveals that this is not the case, that some of the wealthiest individuals in the world have admitted that they never achieved what they really wanted from life.

...But Enough Is Critical.

When more, more, more becomes an obsession, we create all kinds of problems for ourselves. We need food, but more food does not satisfy, fulfill, or provide what we need. Too much, in fact, is destructive to our health. Enough is absolutely necessary for our existence. We need rain, but more rain is not better. Ask flood victims or farmers who have been wiped out when their crops were destroyed by too much rain in too short a period of time. However, enough rain is critical to provide sufficient water for our survival.

We see this principle in every aspect of life. In personal relationships, more time together does not mean two people experience a greater degree of caring or sharing. Enough time, however, is essential to establish and cultivate the relationship.

How Much Is Enough?

The key question, of course, in achieving balance is "How do we know, in the financial area, how much is enough?" One thing is certain; there is no general answer which fits everyone. The personal, specific, and practical question which must be asked is "How much is enough for *you?*" The question and answer become even more personal, specific, and practical when you ask, "How much is enough *today* and how much will it take to be assured that you have enough for *tomorrow?*"

That is where we begin to achieve financial balance. In fact, that is where we begin to achieve balance in our lives.

There is a tendency to judge the quality of values by the dollar signs involved. That would surely be a mistake. As we have seen, more is not better; in the same way, *less* is not necessarily better. There are individuals who have to overcome the belief that making money or acquiring wealth is somehow bad. I am no better or worse because I have more or less.

However, I am only able to experience fulfillment if I have *enough*. While what is enough for me may not be nearly enough for you, it may be far too much for someone else. Enough, defined in very personal, specific, and practical terms, is the key to the whole process. More is not necessarily better, but enough is essential, and the critical question is "How much is enough for *you?*"

Discovering what is right for you, however, is not an easy process. We have difficulty sorting out what we expect for others and what others expect for us. To what extent have we been conditioned by the success or failures of others close to us? Most importantly, if we have difficulty determining what makes us uniquely our own person, we will obviously have difficulty with our money.

We sometimes hear that the Depression shaped the financial attitudes of ourselves, our parents, or our grandparents. Yet there is no simple way to draw a conclusion based on when we were born. There are, for example, individuals today, whether they were born

49

in a bust or boom period in our history, who are now struggling with a lifestyle in which they deprive themselves of the joy of living, and others who overindulge themselves. Even people from very similar backgrounds differ because their reaction to their background has been very different. Recall, for example, from Chapter 2 the difference in the way Joe and Virginia reacted to their similar backgrounds.

Blending Past, Present and Future

It is said that there are three kinds of people; namely, *yesterday* people, *today* people and *tomorrow* people. In that context, where would you put yourself? Perhaps it would help to look at each category briefly.

Now that she has retired from work, Martha tends to live in the past. She remembers with nostalgia the "good old days" when you could purchase a loaf of bread for 10 cents, a new car for a few hundred dollars instead of several thousand, and a new house for several thousand instead of several hundred thousand. From her perspective, things seem to have been better back then. Looking back into history, discovering our "roots," can be extremely useful. We need to know where we have come from. Being a *yesterday* person exclusively, however, prevents Martha from entering into new situations, making new friends to help her enjoy her retirement, or thinking seriously about her future.

Today people concentrate on the here and now. As far as George is concerned, yesterday is gone and there is no tomorrow. Although he recently graduated from college and is just embarking on a teaching career, he feels that planning is a waste of time since no one can really look into the future with any certainty. Instant gratification is his theme song and, although his income is limited, he spends everything he earns on things he wants *now*. Not only does he "celebrate the temporary," he concentrates on the immediate to the exclusion of everything else. The great risk, of course, associated with being a today person is that tomorrow will come and George will be unprepared for it. In fact, for most people, tomorrow does come and the statistics tell us that most people are not prepared.

Eileen, on the other hand, is not only a dreamer, but also spends incredible energy, time and money to get ready for the future—to the exclusion of enjoying today. Since the past can't be relived, she never thinks about it. She ignores her own past. When the suggestion was made that she evaluate how money was spent in her household while she was growing up, she said that she couldn't remember.

For Eileen, even the present is not to be "lived" as much as it is to be used for getting ready to "live." She almost always feels a sense of guilt when she spends money, not on basic necessities, but to have a good time. Consequently, *tomorrow* people such as Eileen run the risk of never getting there, or if they do get there, being unable to enjoy being there. The real question, of course, is "Where is there?" Eileen may never fully enjoy tomorrow unless she is willing to learn that it is a blend of past, present, and future which gives balance and excitement to the process of living.

Financially speaking, we learn from and build upon what we have done in the past with the money we have earned and the capital base we have already built or established; we balance our use of money today between spending to enjoy life (without guilt) and saving/investing (with purpose) for the security and enjoyment of the future. We think about the future and plan for it, anticipating that it will be better than the past and at least as good as today.

A Balanced Life

Henry was a dedicated police officer who retired at the age of 65. Two short years later, he died. Those who knew him believed that he died relatively soon after retiring because, when he quit working, he quit living. All of his life, he had focused on his work in

51

which he took great pride until, in time, it became his reason for living. Although his long tenure had made his future secure and he had achieved financial independence, he was unable to enjoy his independence because he had never developed other interests or close friendships to supplement what he enjoyed on the job. In essence, his financial security was wasted.

For young people, "tomorrow" often seems very far away and unreal. In talking to his father, 17-year-old Tim probably expressed the views of many other students.

"Dad, I don't understand why you're always talking about tomorrow. We don't even know if there will be a tomorrow. Suppose someone pushes the panic button one day and blows the whole world to bits. I'm not going to worry about a future which may not even happen. I'm going to have my fun now."

For the next year, Tim "hung around" with his friends. Since he was a fairly good drummer, what he enjoyed most was being invited to play an occasional gig with a small rock group at local pubs. As playing with the group took more and more time, he soon dropped out of school.

Then, one day, he went to his father again and said, "You know, I've been thinking. What if they don't ever push the panic button and blow the world to bits? What if the world just keeps turning? What if the only thing I can do is play the drums when I'm 30 or 40 or 50 years old? What I really want to do is write songs and maybe work on arrangements. I need to know a lot more about music, though. If you don't mind, I'd like to go back to college and get ready for what I'd enjoy most in the future, just in case I do have a future."

He was the same young man, but with a new sense of purpose. He did go back to college, majored in music, and for the first time, he thoroughly enjoyed what he was doing *and* looked forward to what he might do in the years ahead.

It is amazing how simply by knowing that we are making plans for the future, we feel free to enjoy what we choose to do today. This is what balance is all about.

ACT-I-ON

1. I will make a list of what I am doing to enjoy today.

2. I will make a list of what I am doing to secure tomorrow.

3. I will visualize the tilt of my "balanced living" scale.

4. I will commit (in writing) to make the changes required to achieve the balance I desire.

Mike and Roxanne enjoy being together. They are both great conversationalists and share many of the same ideas about life, although many of their activities are quite different.

Mike, who spends his weekdays indoors as a portfolio manager, really prefers being out-of-doors. He jogs, plays tennis, and loves to go camping in the wilderness. Although he likes his job, he looks forward to weekends and watches the weather report regularly on Friday to plan his weekend activities.

Roxanne is almost obsessed with her career in real estate sales. She is quite successful because she likes working with people, listens well, and follows through to make certain her clients' needs are met. To relax, she reads, watches T.V. or goes to a good movie.

While Mike and Roxanne care very much about each other, they recognize their diverse interests and are feeling pressure to spend more of their time and money doing things that couples "are supposed to do together."

CHAPTER 4

Clarifying Your Life Values

Rating Your Values

All too often, people become mired into a way of living, into behavior patterns, without stopping to ask themselves if they're really getting what they want out of life. Maybe what you have put first in your priorities is not really that important to you. Maybe there are other values that you have pushed to the back of your mind that, in the long run, could bring you greater satisfaction.

That's why financial plans rarely work which address only what people of your age, in your financial bracket, should do with their money. In fact, there does not appear to be any arbitrary system for spending or investing that will work for everyone. The problem with a system is that it doesn't take your pulse or listen to your heartbeat. It doesn't get inside your head. It doesn't respond to who you are or relate to what is unique about you as a person.

So, let me suggest a fun exercise that may start you thinking about the underlying real values in your life. Many people have told us that this was one of the most revealing exercises they had ever done and, moreover, it proved to be a tremendously effective communications vehicle with other people who were important in their lives.

Life Values

This is a sample of 15 key values people typically want to experience for themselves. Some people will experience more of these values than others, but one cannot realize all since some contradict one another.

Assume your situation is such that you HAVE to give up TEN of these values. Which would they be? Drop them out by putting an "X" in the left column.

Now, rank the order for your top five value preferences, from highest (1) to lowest (5). Place your rank order numbers in the left column.

____ Achievement: To accomplish something important in life, be involved in significant activities, succeed at what I am doing.

____ Aesthetics: To be able to appreciate and enjoy beauty for beauty's sake, to be artistically creative.

____ Authority/ Power   To be a key decision-maker directing priorities, the activities of other people and/or allocation and use of general resources.

____ Adventure: To experience variety and excitement, and to be able to respond to challenging opportunities.

____ Autonomy: To be independent, have freedom, be able to live where I want to live and do what I want to do.

____ Health: To be physically, mentally and emotionally well, to feel energetic and maintain a sense of well-being.

____ Integrity: To be honest and straightforward, just and fair.

____ Intimacy/ Friendship/ Love: To have close personal relationships, experience affection, share life with family and friends.

____ Pleasure: To experience enjoyment and personal satisfaction from the activities in which I participate.

____ Recognition: To be seen as successful, receive acknowledgment for achievements.

____ **Security:**	To feel stable and comfortable with few changes or anxieties in my life.
____ **Service:**	To contribute to the quality of life for other people and to be involved in improving society or the world.
____ **Spiritual Growth:**	To have communication or harmony with the infinite source of life.
____ **Wealth:**	To acquire an abundance of money and/or material possessions; to be financially independent.
____ **Wisdom:**	To have insight, be able to pursue new knowledge, have clear judgment and be able to use common sense in life situations.

Think of the exercise you've just done as a starting point only. Looking at the values other people have listed here should bring to mind other values that mean more to you. Substitute your own values if they differ.

Some people may want to make most or all of these values an integral part of their lives. However, what we have to recognize is that when we give emphasis to one of those values, we may have to de-emphasize some of the others. Some may even be in direct conflict with others.

Let me give you an example. Let's say that adventure is very important to you; and so is security.

It's not to say that you can't have both in some kind of balance, but the more emphasis you give to one, the more you are likely to have to give up some of the other. Adventure involves taking some risk, and risk affects your security. The more you settle into a stable, comfortable and secure lifestyle, the less likely you are to experience adventure.

You can certainly pursue pleasure while, at the same time, try to be healthy and wealthy. But chances are one of those three will take a back seat to the other two in the practical arena of your everyday life.

Karen, a highly successful, career-oriented young woman, told us, "I realize that, at this moment in my life, achievement is most important to me.

"I also realize that means, for the time being, I am giving up—or at least postponing—another very important value, which is friendship/intimacy/love. I believe there will still be an opportunity for me to develop those relationships in the future. But for the time being, I'm making them secondary."

What's important here is that Karen knows what her primary value is, recognizes that other values may become more important, and feels comfortable about her priorities.

There is no one who can place a judgment on your life values and tell you that you should value this more than that. You have to decide what you want to achieve in life, and then use your money or other financial resources to make sure that what you value most is realized.

The Financial Planning Pyramid

Managing your money successfully calls not only for a specific life-time plan, but for rooting that plan in a solid foundation.

Most financial pyramids illustrate the importance of risk management being in place, taking care of the basic investment categories first, and then moving to the more aggressive shelters and equities, before finally attempting speculative investments.

I suggest that you might consider another approach to building your own financial plan. What makes the pyramid illustrated in these pages different is that, at the very foundation, there are the words: *personal life values*. Above that is a second fundamental building block: *goals and objectives*, which are based on the foundation established by your personal values.

How you use your money, either for saving or investing, or how basic or speculative you want those investments to be, are decisions that build upon your foundation.

Quite often the financial planning process is short-circuited

Financial Planning Pyramid

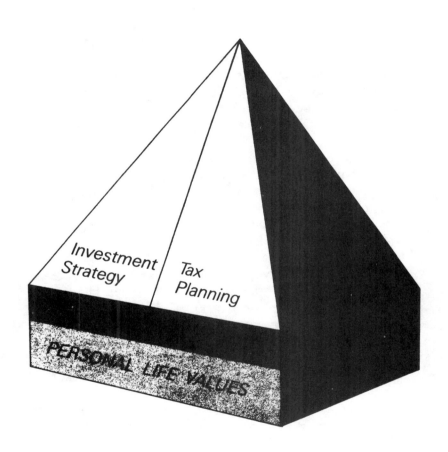

Investment Strategy

Tax Planning

PERSONAL LIFE VALUES

because it doesn't begin at the beginning. We are challenged to answer questions which have to do with the interest rate we are receiving on our invested funds, the taxes we are paying, the amount of insurance coverage and cost thereof, and other details related to the financial facts of our lives. We're challenged also to think about how to increase the rate of return on our investments, reduce our taxes and get more for our money in the field of insurance. While we can see that those may be important, the real question is, why are they important? That takes us back to our goals and objectives. As soon as we begin to examine our goals and objectives, we are back into the base of the financial planning pyramid—our personal life values. Unless we begin there, the process doesn't work.

Let me give you an example. Dr. Wendell, a successful physician, felt that his financial affairs had become exceedingly complex and consulted a professional financial advisor. Early in their first meeting, the advisor asked Dr. Wendell some value clarification questions. The doctor's immediate response was that he placed an extremely high value on life itself; that was what had motivated him to become a physician in the first place. It was important to him not only to be involved in helping to sustain life as existence but to contribute to the other people's quality of life. His greatest feeling of fulfillment came when his knowledge of the newest techniques of medical science enabled him to overturn a situation which had seemed hopeless, and a patient—or sometimes the patient's whole family—responded with a new sense of commitment to living life fully and well. As Dr. Wendell put it, "That's my reason for being."

How then, had he reached the point where he was spending so much money and so much time struggling with personal financial problems?

In looking back, he would tell you today that it was primarily because he never put the base of the pyramid in place before he started the planning process. He had simply listened to someone who said, "Hey, Doc, you're making a lot of money. You need to save on taxes, and you ought to get into this real estate deal that closes next Friday." What he was doing with his money had very little to do with what was important in his life. He was simply responding to peer pressure which says that doctors who earn a lot of money are supposed to invest it. It turned out that some of his investments were questionable, and he became more involved with the Internal Revenue Service than he wanted to be. It was not exactly his idea of how to get the most out of life.

With the assistance of the advisor, Dr. Wendell identified clearly the foundation he wanted for his planning pyramid, and proceeded to develop some creative investment and tax-planning approaches related to his personal life values.

What he discovered was an avenue for investing in medical research and development programs which created both tax advantages and investment growth opportunities for him. More important, he was doing something with his money that he really believed in.

He was also able to set up a retirement program which he could fund aggressively and invest the funds conservatively, with realistic expectations of being able to retire early. This was exciting for him because it would allow him to move eventually from the more demanding surgical practice into the field of medical research. Research had always interested him, and he wanted to be involved in it at a time in his life when he would still be energetic and creative.

The key to the process for Dr. Wendell was beginning at the beginning.

Having a strong sense of self was essential for another physician, Dr. Brower, whose father, now retired, was a surgeon for many years. Through the years, her father has encouraged her to also enter the field of surgery. However, her strong pull is in the direction of chiropractic medicine. She believes in the more holistic approach to health and finds great personal fulfillment in the healing that can be done to some extent with the hands. In terms of her basic personal life values, she feels that she would enjoy chiropractic medicine more than any other aspect of medicine. Yet, it's amazing how many people have reminded her that she would earn much more money in some other field of specialization.

The first hurdle the doctor had to overcome in her life planning and personal financial planning was to get square with herself, with her father and other friendly advisors about what was really important to her. It was only then that she felt free to develop a financial plan that would link realistically to what she wanted to achieve overall.

Differing Values

Several years ago, in one of our seminar/workshops, a young mother-to-be asked a searching question. After completing the goals worksheet, Tammy said, "My husband and I have discovered that our goals are quite different. In fact, it was amazing to us how few of the items on the worksheet we had actually discussed prior to our marriage, and how many areas there are in which we have differing priorities. When we compared our feelings about how we'd like to live in the future, education for our children, saving and investing money, and our willingness to move to pursue career opportunities, we found that our feelings in many instances were miles apart. In my situation (eight months pregnant), we obviously need to be moving in the same direction. How do we deal with our differences?"

While there is no pat answer to Tammy's critical question, raising the question itself is a significant step in the right direction.

Through the years, we all have discovered some fairly basic differences in our values and goals from those of our spouses, business partners or others with whom we are associated. When we focus only on our dollar differences, we too often hit an impasse. When instead, we are able to clarify what is important to each of us (important enough to claim our money), we are better able to resolve differences in an environment of mutual respect and caring. To pretend that this process is easy would be irresponsible. It is, however, possible to integrate our basic lifestyles with decisions we make in every other area of our lives *if* we can get to the core of decision-making: understanding what really matters to us.

Differing Styles

Sometimes, two people have similar goals, but the way in which they approach life may differ.

Eric and Larry, for example, are two young men who recently entered into a business partnership. Their company manufactures microchips using a new technology which they developed. They share similar goals. However, there are some basic differences in the way they prefer to achieve these goals.

Eric is a risk-taker who boasts that he has an entrepreneurial spirit. For Eric, that means that in many instances he is willing to borrow money in order to take advantage of a business opportunity. While he recognizes the possibility that his project may fail, and he would have a debt to repay, he counts on the possibility that his risk-taking will pay off.

Larry, on the other hand, operates on a much more conservative basis. If he has the money in the bank with which to pursue an idea, he may proceed. Otherwise, he will pass on the project.

If it is in their mutual best interests to continue their partnership, Eric and Larry must find a way to accommodate their differences. Otherwise, it may be best to dissolve their partnership and pursue their career opportunities independently.

Again, it's a question of understanding their personal values—which includes how they value their approach to handling life's situations.

63

What Is More Important:
To Me?   To You?

When people disagree about money, they are often disagreeing about differences in values and goals.

Roger, a successful 38-year old corporate executive in a large Southeastern construction firm, has just received a $20,000 bonus. He rushes home and tells the good news to his wife, Katherine, sharing enthusiastically his ideas on what the bonus money will mean to them. First of all, there is the country club membership which Roger has wanted for several years. Then, there is the down payment on a recreational vehicle which he believes will be a great way to bring the family together on short trips. Finally, there is an opportunity to invest in a tax-advantaged investment which a friend has been recommending.

As she listens, Katherine's initial excitement wanes dramatically. The bonus is certainly good news, but she realizes quickly that Roger has already spent the bonus on items which are relatively unimportant to her. For several years, Katherine has dreamed of completing her degree program at the local university and passing the CPA exam. On a part-time basis, she could work with several small corporations and then, when the children were grown, she could secure a full-time career position of her own. However, it will take money as well as time to get the degree.

Roger and Katherine are not in the habit of discussing money. Because they long ago recognized that they had differing attitudes about it, money has become an unpleasant subject—to be avoided if possible.

With the unexpected bonus presenting an immediate challenge, however, Katherine interrupts Roger with an uncharacteristic outburst of her own feelings. "Why can't we use part of the bonus," she asks, "for tuition and babysitting expenses, so I can go back to college and finally become a CPA? And why do we need an RV anyway?" Katherine exclaims. "I'd much rather we take a solid three-week vacation to Europe that we once had talked about."

All of a sudden the good news of the bonus check is diminished. Roger and Katherine argue about how to spend the money. Their voices grow louder and louder as each tries to make one point after another to support differing views.

Roger and Katherine are a good example of a couple who has not yet learned to put money in its place.

What they have not realized is that the subject is not money. The actual subject to be discussed is their values and goals and how money fits in. Even though they have been married for ten years, Roger and Katherine remain distinct individuals. They care, of course, about many of the same things, but their values and goals have not merged.

Now let me tell you the rest of the story. At one point in the discussion, Roger and Katherine were able to stop and ask each other two very basic questions:

1. "What is most important to me?"

2. "What is most important to you?"

It was only then that they were on the way toward dealing with their bonus check, their differences about money, and their relationship.

The result was that Roger did join the country club. Katherine recognized that it was important to him for business as well as personal reasons. Roger became more aware that Katherine's career goals were more serious than he had thought, and she arranged evening courses toward her degree. Roger decided to babysit on one of the evenings each week because, as they talked, he discovered he would welcome a scheduled time to spend with the children. Together, they agreed to forego the recreational vehicle and invest part of the bonus to save for a European trip and/or short family vacations in the future. This time their discussion of money gave each of them a sense of commitment to their shared future.

If the solution seems obvious, the path to reaching it is often difficult. It may mean going into uncharted territory of getting to know yourself and communicating meaningfully with other persons in your life.

Is it worth the effort? Consider the alternative, which is usually far more frustrating and unproductive. Dealing with financial decisions means dealing with your life in a way which gives you choices. There is a sense of power that you are, in large measure, exercising control over your own financial and personal well-being. There are unbelievable possibilities and potential when you make the commitment to get involved. Exploring your own personal values and those of other people in your life may be more rewarding than you realize.

What you may discover is that the amount of money it takes for you to be happy, comfortable, or fulfilled—and how you spend it—may be quite different from that of anyone with whom you share your life. That doesn't make one right and the other wrong. To recognize, accept, and in fact "live" with those differences is what relationships are all about.

The basic point of the financial planning process is that we can put spending (and what we spend on) and saving (and what we save for) in perspective. That is the clearest way to achieve both our individual and shared goals for a life that is fulfilling and rewarding.

ACT-I-ON

1. I will complete the Personal Life Values exercise.

2. I will ask other people who are significant in my life to do the same exercise.

3. I will discuss the results with those who are involved in my decision-making and who are affected by the results of my life planning.

Marilyn and Ed are now in their mid-30's and run a successful catering business. They would like to take one major vacation each year, provide most of the funds for the college education of their three children, keep in reserve a few extra dollars for assisting Ed's mother who is living on Social Security plus a modest pension, and become financially independent at age 60 so they can retire. They have no idea what these goals mean in terms of dollars and cents. Will they really be able to take early retirement, or is it more realistic to think in terms of age 62, 65, or even older?

CHAPTER 5

Your Goals Have Price Tags

Once you've taken the time to recognize what is truly important to you, you can start translating your values and priorities into tangible goals and, even more significantly, into specific financial objectives.

Obviously, our goals may change throughout the course of our lives. That is to be expected. Even our personal values, on which the goals are based, may change.

There are many factors which bring about change: external forces, forces within ourselves, and our situation at various points in our lifespan. Sometimes, the changes are gradual and almost unnoticed. Yet they may have a significant effect. At other times, the changes may be sudden and unexpected.

Whether a specific goal remains the same throughout our lives or changes many times, it is highly motivating to have clearly defined goals in mind. Our lives begin to function more effectively when we realistically set goals and then determine the price tag attached to our goals. That's "putting money in its place."

The Game Of Life

While the challenge of getting your money in place is serious business, I would like to suggest that you look at life as a game. It may help in facing the challenge. There are many applications of this analogy. However, one of the most powerful for planning purposes is to divide life into four quarters, much the same as you would divide the game of football or basketball.

In this four-quarter system, you might consider that there are roughly 20 plus years in each quarter, since life expectancy is probably between 80 and 85 for most of us. This means that when you are 20 or 21 years old, you have finished playing the first quarter in the game of life. Somewhere in your early 40's, you have finished the second quarter which is also the first half. In your early to mid-60's, you have finished the third quarter and begin the fourth and final quarter.

In the game of life, of course, some of us may be fortunate enough to play overtime, and that can be a lot of fun if, in fact, we have planned well and are prepared to experience overtime both emotionally and financially.

One observation which becomes immediately clear is that you can't go back and play any of the quarters over again. Whatever you have learned about the game, of course, you can take into the rest of the game with you. However, the score on the board isn't going to change until you put some new points up there. And you have to do that in the time remaining.

If you were to actually translate life into minutes in an 85-year lifetime, that's about 45 million minutes. And life is not just a scrimmage or practice session. Life is playing the real game every day!

There are several extremely important questions which come to mind when you look at life this way.

First of all, what quarter are you playing right now?

How much time is left on the clock?

What is the score in your particular game of life?

Are you taking time out now and then to review your game plan strategy?

And, if you were given the opportunity, would you be interested in playing overtime?

Just suppose, for a moment, that you live longer than the average life expectancy. You are able to live into your late 80's, 90's or perhaps even to age 100. How would you feel about that? Chances are, you are more likely to be excited about playing overtime if you have learned to play the basic game itself, to have fun and to emerge a winner.

Maybe it's important to ask yourself throughout the game how well you are playing and what strategy is necessary to make you a winner. Now, no one can tell you what it means for you to be a winner in the game of life. However, I think most of us know when we are behind and playing catch up. We also know when we are ahead. We certainly know there is a difference in our game plan strategy based on whether we are playing catch up, or are ahead and continuing to score to stay ahead.

In life, as well as in games, strategy is essential, therefore, and it starts with knowing what you specifically want to achieve. That is, setting goals!

How To Set Goals

It's simple. Right? Just write them down, and be sure that they are personal, specific, and practical. Well, if it is that simple, that's all you need to do. If you can do that, you are fortunate. If, however, you find yourself, like many other people, having difficulty getting started, maybe the following exercise will help. Instead of just sitting there with pen in hand and nothing being written, try this!

Project yourself into the future and picture yourself next year this time.

Where would you like to be?

What would you like to be doing?

How would you like to feel about yourself and what you have accomplished?

What would you list as the most important accomplishments you would like to achieve during the next ten years in these three

71

categories: (1) Financial (2) Career (3) Personal? These do not reflect an order of importance. You should rearrange them, in fact, to indicate what is most important to you.

If you are still having difficulty seeing anything specific in the picture, perhaps some of the following goals which were written down by recent seminar participants may serve as a catalyst for getting you started.

These came from different people and are just ideas of how they began to get personal, specific, and practical. Keep in mind that these did not all come from the same person.

Goals

- Start saving systematically for financial independence

- Set up plan to create funds for college education for two children now age 7 and 10

- Purchase our first home

- Sell my house and move to an apartment nearer my office

- Complete my degree in the career field of my choice

- Join a health club and undertake a regular exercise program

- Learn to play the piano

- Complete my book and submit it to a publisher

- Find a financial advisor with whom I am comfortable and set up a one-year program of planning

- Request departmental transfer to utilize my skills better

- Evaluate my current insurance program—life, disability, medical and property insurance—to determine if coverage is adequate and cost is reasonable

- Retire early and go into business for myself

- Volunteer my services one day a week at the local youth center
- Sell boat (not used anymore) and older car to purchase a new car
- Travel to visit my relatives twice each year
- Sell antiques and invest in income-producing assets
- Provide for continuity of income in event of disability
- Update will to reflect current wishes in event of my death
- Completely replace my wardrobe to reflect the "new me"
- Take the entire family on a 10-day vacation
- Buy the lake property to build a retirement cottage later.

As you can see, some of these goals are career-oriented, involve financial planning, or reflect personal aspirations. Some combine goals in two areas; others will bring about satisfaction in all three.

What about *your* goals? Can you define them for the next year or two? For the next ten?

At this point, think of all the things you would really like to accomplish. Since most of us are unable to accomplish everything we might list, however, the next step is to examine what is most important to us. Ask yourself:

"If I could accomplish only one major goal this year, what would it be?"

Turn it around now, and ask, "If I had to give up one activity or one thing right now, what would that be?"

You might then make certain that what matters most is at the top of your list. What is least important can be eliminated. This process enables you to ascribe realistic priorities to your goals and focus on what you need to do to achieve them.

Setting Objectives

It may be helpful to distinguish between goals and objectives. You start by identifying a goal and, then, your objective is your course of action to accomplish that goal.

For example, a goal might be to educate your children, and an objective would state the amount of money that you will have to create in order to educate your children. A goal might be to achieve financial independence by the time you're age 60. In terms of objectives, you would then set specific percentages of income that you would save to create a certain amount of income beginning at age 60.

Let's look again at those goals listed by the seminar participants. This time, let's add an assumed price tag to achieve each goal. This is the beginning of the process of establishing objectives.

Let's also add a third important part of the process-having a target date or reasonable time line for getting the job done.

Stated simply, if I know what I want, know what it takes to get it, and know when I want it, I can then determine whether or not my goal is realistic. Moreover, I can determine whether or not it truly reflects the priority I've given it from my personal life values.

GOALS	PRICE TAG	TARGET DATE
Start saving systematically for financial independence	10% of salary	begin immediately; continue through age 60
Set up plan to create funds for college education for two children ages 7 and 10	approx. $30,000 each in today's dollars	begin immediately for availability of full amount in 10 years
Purchase first home	$120,000	6 months to one year from today
Sell my house and move to an apartment nearer my office	house sale net equity should be $100,000; apartment will cost $750 per month	begin now; complete as soon as possible; invest sale proceeds to get net return equal to cost of apartment if possible
Sell boat and older car to purchase new car	$3,000 plus the value of old car and boat	3 months from now
Travel to visit my relatives twice each year	$2,000 per year	begin this summer
Sell antiques and invest in income-producing assets	no cost; will gain	income by end of this year
Provide for continuity of income in event of disability	$1,200 per year approx.	immediately

GOALS	PRICE TAG	TARGET DATE
Update will to reflect current wishes in event of my death	approx. $300 for legal fees	within 60 days
Completely replace my wardrobe to reflect the "new me"	$5,000	within the next 30 days
Take the entire family on a 10-day vacation	$5,500	late summer this year
Buy the lake property for later retirement cottage	$20,000	within the next 18 months
Complete my degree in the career field of my choice	$4,000	begin this fall; complete in 2 yrs.
Complete my book and submit it to a publisher	approx. $1,000 for typing service	in next 12 months
Join a health club and begin regular exercise program	$300	this week
Learn to play the piano	$100 a month	this year
Find a financial advisor with whom I am comfortable and set up a one-year program of planning	unknown- up to several thousand dollars	ASAP, begin now
Evaluate current insurance program-life, disability, medical and property insurance -to determine if coverage is adequate and cost is reasonable	unknown	within next 30 days
Request departmental transfer to utilize my skills better	0	immediately
Retire early and go into business for myself	unknown-need to determine	5 years from now
Volunteer my services one day a week at the local youth center	0	begin now

As I indicated, this was a list covering the goals of many different people. What it indicates, however, is the diversity of goals possible in several key areas of people's lives. For people with multiple important goals, priorities will have to be set and a timetable established.

By deciding, however, what is important to us, and putting an appropriate price tag on our preferred lifestyle, we have taken a major step in understanding how money and our values go together. We are well on our way toward "putting money in its place."

A Common Goal: Financial Independence

Everyone does not have retirement as a goal. Some people intend to continue working at their business, job or profession as long as they live.

When we understand the benefit of financial independence, however, that becomes a common goal for all of us, whether or not we ever retire. Financial independence enables us to look at our work and our leisure from a new perspective. It enables us to do whatever we choose with our lives. It gives us freedom to be as creative as we are capable of being with our time, energy and talent. Inadequate financial resources restrict us. Having enough money to supply what we need for the rest of our lives releases the brakes and allows us to accelerate at our own pace. If we want to slow down, we can. If we want to work harder than ever, we can do that, without the concern of having to earn money for the basics of our lifestyle.

Max and Coleen enjoy their work and do not feel they will ever retire. They talk about what they will be doing in their respective careers when they are in their eighties. Both of them, though, are committed to a plan which will enable them, at about age 60, to back away and take a fresh look at their respective careers and lifestyles. If they continue with their planning each year as they have projected, they will be financially independent in their early 60's.

At that time, Max may turn more of his attention to consulting on a volunteer basis with one of the community agencies. Coleen enjoys participating in a program designed for young athletes who aspire to national competition. Her role as a psychologist is very effective in helping teenagers develop the mental discipline required. She has found her own devotion to physical fitness a real asset in working with young athletes, and believes she could make a significant contribution when she is 60. Her own financial independence will offer the opportunity to become as involved as she desires. It's exciting for both Max and Coleen to think about the expanded alternatives in the future which financial independence will bring. Yet neither of them is making plans to retire.

We talked earlier about "balanced living"- enjoying today while planning for the security of tomorrow. Let's examine in personal, specific and practical terms what is involved in achieving a lifestyle that balances the present and the future.

The first step is to determine what your preferred lifestyle is for today and the price tag attached. What does it cost for you to do the things you choose to do now?

Secondly, make any adjustments you feel are appropriate for changes in your lifestyle at the time in the future when you would like to be independent financially. The changes could be very minor or they could be drastic, depending upon what you envision for the future. In order to plan realistically, try to be as honest as you can about what you would prefer, if funds were available, yet not wild and unreasonable.

In order to take into account the effect of inflation on your cost of living, turn to the inflation chart on page 78. Determine the price tag in today's dollars for your preferred lifestyle at your projected age of independence. Then multiply that figure by the factor for inflation at an estimated annual percentage rate for the number of years between your present age and the age at which you hope to become financially independent.

Let's look at an example of how this process works.

Kimberly is 40 years old and would like to be financially independent by the time she reaches age 60. That's 20 years from now. Her estimate for inflation is an annual increase in the cost of living of about 3.5%. Using the chart, you can see that the factor for 20 years at 3.5% is approximately 2.0. That means the dollars it would take today for her to experience her projected lifestyle at 60

77

INFLATION CHART

Annual Rate Of Inflation

Years	2%	3%	4%	5%	6%	7%	8%	9%	10%	12%
1	1.02	1.03	1.04	1.05	1.06	1.07	1.08	1.09	1.10	1.12
2	1.04	1.06	1.08	1.10	1.12	1.14	1.17	1.19	1.21	1.25
3	1.06	1.09	1.12	1.16	1.19	1.23	1.26	1.30	1.33	1.40
4	1.08	1.13	1.17	1.22	1.26	1.31	1.36	1.41	1.46	1.57
5	1.10	1.16	1.22	1.28	1.34	1.40	1.47	1.54	1.61	1.76
6	1.13	1.19	1.27	1.34	1.42	1.50	1.59	1.68	1.77	1.97
7	1.15	1.23	1.32	1.41	1.50	1.61	1.71	1.83	1.95	2.21
8	1.17	1.27	1.37	1.48	1.59	1.72	1.85	1.99	2.14	2.48
9	1.20	1.30	1.42	1.55	1.69	1.84	2.00	2.17	2.36	2.77
10	1.22	1.34	1.48	1.63	1.79	1.97	2.16	2.37	2.59	3.11
11	1.24	1.38	1.54	1.71	1.90	2.10	2.33	2.58	2.85	3.48
12	1.27	1.43	1.60	1.80	2.01	2.25	2.52	2.81	3.14	3.90
13	1.29	1.47	1.67	1.89	2.13	2.41	2.72	3.07	3.45	4.36
14	1.32	1.51	1.73	1.98	2.26	2.58	2.94	3.34	3.80	4.89
15	1.35	1.56	1.80	2.08	2.40	2.76	3.17	3.64	4.18	5.47
16	1.37	1.60	1.87	2.18	2.54	2.95	3.43	3.97	4.59	6.13
17	1.40	1.65	1.95	2.29	2.69	3.16	3.70	4.33	5.05	6.87
18	1.43	1.70	2.03	2.41	2.85	3.38	4.00	4.72	5.56	7.69
19	1.46	1.75	2.11	2.53	3.03	3.62	4.32	5.14	6.12	8.61
20	1.49	1.81	2.19	2.65	3.21	3.87	4.66	5.60	6.73	9.65
21	1.52	1.86	2.28	2.79	3.40	4.14	5.03	6.11	7.40	10.80
22	1.55	1.92	2.37	2.93	3.60	4.43	5.44	6.66	8.14	12.10
23	1.58	1.97	2.46	3.07	3.82	4.74	5.87	7.26	8.95	13.55
24	1.61	2.03	2.56	3.23	4.05	5.07	6.34	7.91	9.85	15.18
25	1.64	2.09	2.67	3.39	4.29	5.43	6.85	8.62	10.83	17.00
30	1.81	2.43	3.24	4.32	5.74	7.61	10.06	13.27	17.45	29.96
35	2.00	2.81	3.95	5.52	7.69	10.68	14.79	20.41	28.10	52.80

will double over the next 20 years if the cost of living does go up by an average of 3.5% per year. Let's say she feels that if she spent about $30,000 per year at age 60, she would be able to do the things she enjoys most. With 20 years to go before she gets there, the actual dollars required (based on 3.5% inflation rate) at age 60 would be $60,000 for the first year. That figure is the result of multiplying $30,000 by 2.0 (the factor from the chart).

Obviously, it would be unrealistic for Kimberly to plan on $30,000 at age 60 unless inflation completely disappears.

Now, let's look beyond age 60.

Unfortunately, inflation doesn't automatically quit just because we quit working. If it is a factor for Kimberly for the next 20 years, it will most likely continue to be a factor from age 60 on. What if inflation continues each year at the same 3.5% per year for the rest of Kimberly's life?

At age 61 she will need 60,000 x 1.035 or $62,100 to support the same lifestyle, and the next year, at age 62, the 3.5% increase will mean $64,274, is needed (62,100 x 1.035) and so on. There are computerized programs designed to project income needs for each year of your life and to determine the investment funds or capital required to provide that income. This is where a professional advisor can be extremely valuable in helping you analyze your need.

Let me give you an idea, though, of the challenge for Kimberly. In order to have income at age 60 of $60,000 the first year and 3.5% more each year for the rest of her life, if she assumed her investments would earn a return on average each year equal to inflation (3.5%) she would need to multiply $60,000 the number of years she expects to live. If Kimberly expects to live to age 85 and wants to be financially independent at age 60, that means a goal for Kimberly of about 1.5 million dollars. The equation is $60,000 x 25 years for a total of $1,500,000. The actual computation is somewhat complex, but when the investment rate of return and inflation are basically equal, you can determine the investment capital required by multiplying the income needed the first year of financial independence by the number of years you expect to live. Keep in mind that Kimberly has the next 20 years to achieve her goal of accumulating 1.5 million dollars.

Let's take another example in order to illustrate the impact of inflation on the planning process. Vernon is 65 years old and asking himself if he has achieved financial independence yet. Could he retire today if he wanted to, or would he have to continue working or earning extra money in some way in order to live the way he wants to live?

Vernon believes he can be happy with about $34,000 this year. He has finally paid off the mortgage on his home and doesn't have very many obligations beyond his basic expenses for living. He enjoys going places and doing things, but isn't extravagant in his lifestyle. If Vernon projected income for another 20 years, and assumed his invested funds would keep pace with inflation each year, he would need $600,000 today in order to be financially independent (30,000 x 20 years = $600,000).

What Kimberly and Vernon have in common is a lifestyle with a price tag that is similar in today's dollars. What makes their goal dramatically different is that Vernon is 65 years old and hoping he has achieved independence financially, while Kimberly's goal is 20
years away. While inflation makes the dollars much greater for Kimberly (about 1.5 million of capital compared to Vernon's need for' $600,000). Kimberly has 20 years of time in which to accumulate the assets needed. Vernon needs to have $600,000 financial resources available today. The remainder of the calculation and planning process involves an analysis of the after-tax value of investment assets, company benefits, retirement programs and other financial resources either available today or projected into the future.

In both examples, the funds required to be financially independent will vary, based on the assumptions regarding inflation and the investment rate of return in comparison to inflation. You can, however, very quickly begin to understand and appreciate the challenge when you get involved in the planning process.

Making Your Goals Personal

How you feel about things is very personal; so are the goals you set. As much as we might like to put our values into someone else's life, even if it's only because we want to help them, it just doesn't work that way. I cannot decide what is important for you, and I would not let you decide that for me. That is something each of us has to do individually.

Luke is a man I knew who clearly illustrates the point that we cannot transfer our goals to anyone else.

When he was a young man, he dreamed of being a lawyer. His family had a limited income, and Luke worked hard — in school and in part-time jobs. He put himself through college, and the proudest moment of his life was when he learned he had been accepted into a prestigious law school.

Unfortunately, during his first year at the school, Luke's father died. Luke was suddenly faced with the agonizing decision to drop out of law school and find a job to help take care of his mother and younger sisters.

An uncle took him into his real estate business. Eventually, as Luke learned more about the business, he began to enjoy it and do well. In time, he established his own real estate firm and did exceedingly well financially.

In the back of his mind, however, there always lingered a regret that he had not had a chance to become the lawyer he had dreamed of being.

Luke's son, Jonathan, grew up in an environment in which it was clear that since the law was an essential part of a civilized society, attorneys were an especially valuable segment of that society in upholding the law. Through the years, Luke never thought of asking Jonathan about his career interests; he assumed that since his financial success would make it possible for his son to go through law school, Jonathan would, of course, want to take advantage of being able to become an attorney.

Unfortunately, Jonathan did not know how — or wasn't given the opportunity — to get in touch with his own personal values well enough to communicate effectively with his father. He went along with his father's plans and finished law school.

On the day he received his diploma, Jonathan handed it to his father and said, "Here, Dad, you wanted this, you got it."

For Jonathan, however, there was no real interest in practicing law, and he never did.

81

Had the father and son been able to discuss their own personal values, this misdirection of Jonathan's time and energies might never have happened. The focus was in the wrong place—to realize a goal which was set for one person by another person without any clear communication regarding each other's personal values.

Planning Involves Other People

Few individuals can do either their life planning or financial planning in isolation. Most of us share life in some way with other people to the extent that our decisions affect them and, invariably, their decisions affect us.

That is the reason communication is so important. Often we need to find agreement or, failing that, negotiate our differences, make appropriate compromises, and arrive at a solution about how best to share our lives and our money.

Active listening is a skill which can benefit us tremendously and can add unbelievable results to the process of our own planning.

Perhaps you already know how to listen attentively. However, if you feel that you would like to improve your listening skills, you might want to try this experiment.

Sit down with someone who is involved in your life, and take turns listening. One of you talk, and the other listen for at least five minutes. Then switch the listening and talking roles.

It is important to get immediate feedback. Ask your partner in this communication exercise if you heard accurately what he or she has said. If not, try again.

While this exercise makes you more aware of how well we really listen to what people are trying to tell us, it also gives an opportunity to talk, to open up to those we care about, and learn to express and articulate our feelings and ideas.

Enjoy The Process

Finally, something which can help tremendously is to relax and let yourself enjoy the goal-setting process. If reaching goals is fun, so is the planning.

Planning is obviously important, and it is serious business. However, it should also be fun. Chances are that if we enjoy the process of planning, we'll be more willing to be involved in it and be more effective.

Regardless of your goals, *if you don't have fun getting there, the chances are you won't have fun being there.*

ACT-I-ON

1. I will list my goals.

2. I will put a pricetag on each goal.

3. I will set a realistic target date for achieving each goal.

4. I will discuss/negotiate with my mate/children/parents or other significant people in my life each goal which affects them.

Vince, a computer programmer, is approaching his 40th birthday. He has been divorced for four years, and is still making child support payments. He recently became engaged to a young divorced woman, who also has a child from a previous marriage, and is excited about doing some serious planning for the future.

His immediate problem is that he doesn't really know where he is today. The last financial statement he put together was for the bank when he borrowed money for a cottage at the lake. He saves a little money, but doesn't actually keep any records to speak of. Although he participates in all of the company benefit programs, he doesn't know what the benefits actually mean in terms of future planning. In order to play the rest of the game strategically, Vince needs to know the score today.

CHAPTER 6

Time Out—What's The Score?

This is the beginning of the process of developing a financial plan tailor-made to *your* goals: knowing what your resources are.

To illustrate somewhat absurdly, if you have virtually no assets today, are earning a meager income and lack the entrepreneurial spirit, but dream of becoming financially independent next year, your inventory doesn't support the dream. Miracles can happen, and that's what it would take for your dream to come true. This is the posture of people who keep hoping the next lottery ticket or trip to Las Vegas will magically solve their financial dilemma.

The good news, however, is that even with virtually no assets, but an earned income and a commitment to balance the enjoyment of the present with the future, there is reason to anticipate a day when you can realistically be financially independent. It may not be as soon as you would like, but it is possible, and the journey can be exciting and rewarding.

Taking inventory involves knowing where you are today. It also involves projecting where you want to be in the future, and calculating what is required to get there.

You may need assistance in the actual calculations, or in determining the projected value of your investment assets, of pension, profit-sharing or other benefit plans, and that's where professional advisors can help. You are in a better position to ask real questions and get real answers, however, if you "have a feel for the process."

Gathering Information

In pulling together the information which indicates your financial resources, you may want to start by accumulating the various documents which are part of your financial picture. On page 89 is a Personal Document Checklist. Use it as a reminder of the different kinds of documents you will find helpful, such as personal papers, financial statements, tax returns, etc.

Next, although it may take a while to do this, it can be a very valuable use of your time to sit down and make a list of all of your company and personal benefits. Include items such as insurance, retirement plans, stock programs, deferred compensation arrangements and any other benefits.

Finally, you definitely need to take inventory of what you have done in terms of a basic will or trust arrangement. What are your plans for the distribution of your assets in the event of your death?

If you don't have a will which has been written to express your desires and wishes, there is one that has been written for you. It exists in the probate law in the court house in the state in which you live. It is a very arbitrary arrangement for distributing your assets which has been set up by the laws of the state for those who don't get around to putting their own wills in writing.

Be sure, too, that your will is readily accessible. A will, for example, which you are certain you signed years ago, but cannot locate, is of no value unless available at the time it is needed. Therefore, if it cannot be located, you would be well advised to prepare a new will and revoke all past wills.

Once you have identified all those papers which are applicable in your situation, it is important to either locate them and have them available, or determine that they do not exist or have been lost and need to be reconstructed.

A Balance Sheet For Planning

One of the ways we determine the score today is to take a

Personal Document Checklist

☐ Tax Returns

☐ Financial Statement — Current

☐ Trust Documents

☐ Agreements Still in Effect

☐ Employment Paycheck Stubs

☐ Contracts, Deeds, Notes, and Leases

☐ Investments

☐ Medical Insurance

☐ Previous Analyses

☐ Retirement Plans

☐ Disability Insurance

☐ Property/Liability Insurance

☐ Life Insurance

"snapshot" of our current net worth. Ordinarily, one can simply subtract the liabilities from the assets and determine one's net worth fairly easily. Undoubtedly, you've done that in the past, but let's try now to do it a little differently.

A truly helpful balance sheet enables you to separate your *personal* assets and liabilities from your *investment* assets and liabilities.

So, the bottom line is that you have two net worths. You have a personal net worth and an investment net worth. That's a very important distinction to make in the financial planning process.

If you haven't done this exercise recently, you need to put together a balance sheet, and make this distinction.

First of all, let me restate why that's important. As we accumulate assets through the years, we make decisions about where to put our money. Many people begin with things such as personal property, automobiles, clothing and household furnishings. Most of those fall in the category of personal assets. We may also put some money into various kinds of investments to create assets for our future income.

If we walked down the street and asked people the question, "What is the best investment you've ever made?" what do you think most people would reply? That's right. Most people would say, "My home." Let's take a look at that, however. If the house you live in today is the house you will be living in for the rest of your life, is it really an investment? Does it matter, in fact, what that house is worth? Now, if you live in a large home today and you plan one day to sell it and buy a smaller, less expensive home, or if you plan to sell your house and rent in your later years, then it may be that the value of your home can be included as an investment. That's a personal decision. And it's one that needs to be made as you look at your own situation and determine what makes sense to you.

One of my neighbors, Margaret, once said to me that the best investment she and her husband had ever made was a lot, a piece of undeveloped land. They paid $5,000 for it and today they could sell it for $100,000. I asked her if she planned to sell it. "Of course not," Margaret said. "That's where we are going to build our retirement home." Well, if the lot is the location for their retirement home, it isn't going to be an investment, is it? It may be worth a lot of money, but it doesn't produce any income unless they are willing to sell it.

Let's take a look at the balance sheet now, and examine the way you put the figures together in the various columns. We're using an abbreviated version of the traditional balance sheet just to get an idea of how this works. Michelle and Jerry, participants at one of our seminars, put their figures together for us.

Balance Sheet

	I PERSONAL	II INVESTMENT	III TOTAL
Assets			
Cash/Savings	$ 1,000	$ 10,000	$ 11,000
Stocks/Bonds		20,000	20,000
Real Estate	100,000	75,000	175,000
Other	25,000	30,000	55,000
Total Assets	$126,000	$135,000	$261,000

First of all, there is a listing of their assets in either the personal or the investment column. Then, in the third column, there is the total. In this case, they are saying that the total of cash and savings is $11,000. There's about $1,000 in cash which is just personal money and $10,000 in savings earmarked for investment.

On the second line, stocks and bonds—a total of $20,000—are listed, all of it investment.

On the real estate line, they have two items.

Under the personal column—$100,000. They are estimating that this is the value of their home—a home in which they intend to continue to live.

In the investment column, they have $75,000. That is designated as real estate for investment purposes.

The total, then, on the real estate line is $175,000.

They have listed, as "other" under the personal column, $25,000. That might consist of automobiles, clothing, furniture, etc. In the investment column the $30,000 is "other kinds of assets" such as investment in the categories of oil and gas, gold, silver, etc. It might also include the cash value in their life insurance programs. The total, then, of the other items is $55,000.

So you can see, in this example, the personal assets consist of a total of $126,000. The investment assets, $135,000. The total assets are $261,000.

Now, let's take a look at the liabilities portion of the balance sheet. Again, we have the three columns. Under the liabilities, they list the mortgages. Against that $100,000 home, there is a $60,000 mortgage. And in the investment column against the $75,000 real estate values, there are $35,000 of mortgages. So they have a total of $95,000 in mortgages.

There are personal loans of $5,000 and investment loans of $10,000, giving them total loans of $15,000. They have credit card obligations of $1,000 and that goes in the personal column. They didn't plug in any figures in the "other" column, but those could consist of things such as personal loans from relatives, or other liabilities that they have created personally. In the investment column, they might also have additional liabilities which would not fall in the categories of mortgages, loans, or credit cards.

Balance Sheet

	I PERSONAL	II INVESTMENT	III TOTAL
Liabilities			
Mortgages	$60,000	$35,000	$ 95,000
Loans	5,000	10,000	15,000
Credit Cards	1,000		1,000
Other			
Total Liabilities	$66,000	$45,000	$111,000

Balance Sheet

	PERSONAL	INVESTMENT	TOTAL
Assets	$126,000	$135,000	$261,000
Liabilities	66,000	45,000	111,000
Net Worth Personal	60,000		
Investment		90,000	
Total			150,000

Their totals in the personal column are liabilities of $66,000, investment liabilities of $45,000, and a total of $111,000.

Now let's look at the third chart for the balance sheet. That's the summary. Here, we take the figures we have just discussed and pull them forward. Personal assets, $126,000; liabilities, $66,000. So Michelle and Jerry have a personal net worth of $60,000. With investment assets of $135,000, and liabilities against those investment assets of $45,000, their investment net worth is $90,000.

Now think about this. When you complete a typical balance sheet, if these were your figures, you would show your net worth as the figures in the column, would you not? Assets of $261,000, liabilities of $111,000, total net worth $150,000.

The Critical Point

What is absolutely critical, at this point, is to recognize that although Michelle and Jerry are in a position to demonstrate a net worth of $150,000, for planning purposes, when they look into the future and talk about retirement or total financial independence, they only have $90,000 for that purpose. The other $60,000 of net worth is invested in things which they are using personally and have decided that they are going to continue to use personally.

Keep in mind that this is not a judgmental exercise. It's not designed to say you should do this or you should do that. It is intended to help you clarify what the facts really mean in your own situation and how you can use those facts to accomplish what's important to you.

What we've discovered is that this balance sheet for planning creates all kinds of new opportunities for decision-making.

You can't make responsible decisions—decisions that give you a sense of freedom to spend without guilt, and to save with purpose—unless you have accurate information in front of you. By using this kind of balance sheet, you can have a more realistic view of what resources you really have available.

A Plan For Spending

Next, you need to take a picture of your cash flow. That means asking "What do I have coming in?" and "Where is it going?" In many situations, people may not even know what's coming in—in terms of income—or where it is going. It's easy in the hurried way we live to get so busy that we just don't pay attention to the flow of our cash. It just seems to flow away.

What *are* your receipts and your expenditures? That should be an actual history of accounting to yourself for the way you spend your money. It is probably far more valuable for most people to develop an actual *spending plan* than it is for them to create a *hypothetical budget*. Very few budgets become operative. So, instead, look realistically at where you are actually spending your money.

It is possible to think we are saving money when we are not saving any *new* money at all. It's critical, for example, when we do make investments, that we look at the importance of reinvesting what our investments produce.

Let me give you an example that will help you see how dynamic this simple exercise can be in the decision-making in your own life.

Here is a cash flow statement which shows that the total income

Cash Flow

Personal Service Income	$50,000	
Investment Income	$ 5,000	
Total Income		$55,000
Lifestyle Expenses		$53,000
Net Cash Flow		$ 2,000

for Ron and Debbie is $55,000. The total lifestyle expense for them is $53,000. So it appears that the net cash flow is $2,000, doesn't it? They might say to themselves, "We have $55,000 coming in, we are only spending $53,000, so we are saving $2,000 a year." But, let's break that down a little more carefully.

When you look more closely at the figures, you see that the personal service income (that is salaries, wages, what we used to call earned income) is a total of $50,000, and the investment income is $5,000. Looking at the second chart, we take the $50,000 of personal service income and subtract the lifestyle expenses of $53,000. So actually the net cash flow is a minus or negative $3,000.

Cash Flow

Personal Service Income	$50,000
Lifestyle Expenses	53,000
Net Cash Flow	(3,000)
Other Receipts:	
Investment Income	$ 5,000
Net Income Reinvested	$ 2,000

In this situation, Ron and Debbie are not saving any *new* money at all. They are spending the total of the $50,000 that they are making from their personal service, and an additional $3,000 that is income from their investments. Therefore, part of the investment income is already being used to support today's lifestyle. Only $2,000 of the $5,000 investment income is actually being reinvested each year.

To bring this down to the practical bottom line of what difference it makes, let's look at the final set of figures. The question is: what is the cost of using investment income to support your lifestyle today? If that $5,000 coming from investments were re-invested each year at 6% per year for 20 years, it would accumulate to a total of $183,928.

Cost of Using Investment Income
(To Support Lifestyle)

$5,000 @ 6% for 20 years =	$183,928
$2,000 @ 6% for 20 years =	73,571
	$110,357

If, however, you only had $2,000 per year to re-invest as we illustrated in our example here, that $2,000 each a year for the next 20 years at 6% will only grow to $73,571. The difference is $110,357.

So, in summary, it will cost Ron and Debbie over $110,000 in terms of future security for them to use a portion of their investment income today to support their current lifestyle.

Again, there is no judgment at all intended here. What is important is that this exercise can be useful in your own planning. If you know what's coming in and you know where it's going, you will be much better able to use your money to get what you want out of life.

Taxes

Let's look next at your *tax situation*. There are basically three things that you should know about your tax picture. One, your taxable income; two, your cumulative tax that has to be paid on that taxable income; and three, the progressive tax rate at which you are paying your taxes. That's the way you actually discover your top *marginal tax bracket*.

And that is a very *important* piece of information for you to have. It should, in fact, be taken into consideration in all of your financial decisions. If someone suggests that you move money from a taxable account to a tax-free account, for example, how could you possibly know if that's a wise decision unless you are aware of your top marginal tax bracket?

What you've just done in the information-gathering process should help you begin to clearly answer the question "Where am I today" and prepare you for the next big question: "What should I do with what I've got to get what I want out of life?"

ACT-I-ON

1. I will complete a current balance sheet in order to take a "snapshot" of my investment net worth today.

2. I will create a realistic "spending plan."

Lisa, a 34-year-old widow with two children, works as a nurse at her local general hospital. She does not like making decisions. She enjoys doing research on various projects, but would prefer someone else take the responsibility for the final decisions. In her financial life, therefore, many important decisions never get made.

Janet, at 28, is extremely comfortable making decisions. That's the nature of her job as an office manager. However, she doesn't feel she has the time to look at all the alternatives and evaluate the various advantages and disadvantages of financial decisions. Yet, whom can she trust to objectively bring to her the information she needs?

CHAPTER 7

You're Calling The Signals

Once we have put our personal life values in place and have established goals and objectives based on those values, decision-making becomes somewhat easier. We have already accomplished much by weeding out alternatives which do not make sense for us. We have narrowed the field considerably to include only those options which are more appropriately based on who we are and what we are trying to achieve with our money. Additional groundwork has been laid in setting priorities as we examined the balance between our needs for today and our needs for the future. And, finally, we prepared for the decision-making process by taking realistic inventory.

In the final analysis, however, no matter how much thinking and feeling and planning we do, unless we make decisions—and take action on those decisions—nothing really changes.

To get the results we are looking for, therefore, we've reached the point where we finally have to do something.

Coordinating The Process

The first major decision you need to make is whether you would prefer orchestrating the decision-making and implementation process yourself. If not, should you find a primary trusted advisor who can coordinate the process for you?

To do it on your own, you must feel that you have the time and are capable of communicating with each of the various professionals who are involved in your financial situation.

If *you* manage the planning process, you will have to meet with your insurance representative to discuss your insurance needs and make an informed decision about your insurance program. You will meet with your attorney regarding wills, trusts and other legal matters, with your accountant regarding tax matters, and with your investment broker and other specialists whom you may need to call upon. Most importantly, you will need the expertise to be able to pull together all of their various recommendations and integrate those into a total financial program which will meet your objectives. If there are inconsistencies, gaps or overlaps, you will have to make a decision on how to resolve them.

Historically, most people have found this process to be a somewhat overwhelming challenge. In fact, that is the primary reason for the emergence of a new profession over the last two decades. While that profession is still evolving, it is represented by professional individuals and planning firms committed to serving as primary trusted advisors who coordinate the financial planning process. They have the expertise to work closely with clients and with other professionals who are needed by the client for the decision-making and implementation process.

In a later chapter, we will discuss more fully where and how to select a professional financial advisor and the various other advisors in the financial services field. The point here is that you have a major decision to make up front: will you serve as your own coordinator, or will you select someone who can work closely with you to develop your plan? The more complicated your situation is and the more you have at stake, the more you may wish to use someone who can assist you. A primary trusted advisor, who is well-trained, is prepared to offer comprehensive services—from clarifying your personal life values, to monitoring your progress through periodic reviews of your situation, to advising on decisions when changes are required. Keep in mind, however, that the final test is that your system works for you.

Let's look now at several typical areas in which financial decisions may be required in order to illustrate some of the steps in decision-making. Very often, one decision involves many other decisions along the way. Buying a place in which to live, for example.

Deciding Where To Live

Elizabeth's situation is a fairly typical one in today's society. Most of the principles which are illustrated would apply whether the purchaser of a home is a young man/young woman, young couple just starting out, a middle-aged person or couple buying a second or third home, older people choosing a retirement home, or any individual whose circumstances differ from Elizabeth's, but whose decision and action involve the purchase of a place in which to live.

Elizabeth, a personnel director in her late forties, is thinking of buying a condominium in an urban area fairly close to her work. When she was first married, she and her husband worked in town. But when their children came along, they moved to suburbia. Elizabeth gave up her job to become a full-time mother, while her husband commuted back and forth from the city. For the past 10 years, however, she too has been working in the city—and commuting. Now, her family situation has changed, and she lives alone again.

In recent years, her job has turned into a much more challenging career. Taking almost two hours out of every day to get to and from her office does not seem to be a good use of her time. In addition, the friends with whom she now shares social activities live in the downtown area. The question is, how does she go about making her decision to purchase a condominium near her work. Let's look at some of the primary considerations.

First of all, Elizabeth has to decide, either in concert with her primary financial advisor or based on her own knowledge of her financial situation, the price range she can afford. It can be a fairly broad range, but she will save considerable time and emotional energy if she determines, at the outset, what is realistic. It can be extremely frustrating, for example, to find an exciting condominium, in just the right development, with all of the amenities, only to discover that there is one major barrier—a price tag which she absolutely cannot afford. It is also possible that she might consider juggling funds to acquire something outside her price range, but this may call for sacrifices in other areas which she would later regret.

What Elizabeth wants to do at this point is guard against being tempted to make an emotional decision. She does that by coming up with a realistic price range and then doing her condominium shopping accordingly.

It will be helpful also for her to make a list of the related advantages or disadvantages which are important to her such as:

1. Transportation time to and from work

2. The security features of the condominium complex

3. Ability to have pets, if important

4. Extra bedrooms for guests

5. Aesthetics such as the outside and inside appearance of the building, the view and the general neighborhood

6. Features of the condominium which are important in terms of her lifestyle, including such items as dishwasher, disposal, washer/dryer, closet space, tennis courts, pool, jogging area, etc.

7. Any other features or amenities which she considers important to enable her to be comfortable and to feel good about where she lives.

Elizabeth's choice will be somewhat easier if she also checks off which items on this list are most/least important to her.

The importance of finding a real estate specialist who knows the local condominium market well cannot be overemphasized. If Elizabeth has time and enjoys doing some of the scouting on her own, that's fine. However, there will come a time when she will need someone she trusts to give her accurate information and to help her make that final decision. There are knowledgeable, competent people in the real estate field who will go beyond answering questions to provide valuable insights about the town, neighborhoods, tax rates, water and sewage system, the local government, and recent developments.

Finally, there are the terms of the actual financial transaction. And this may be a point at which Elizabeth should consult either her primary financial advisor, if she has one, or a trusted loan officer at a financial institution, to learn what terms are available and what terms are best for Elizabeth based on her financial status.

There is usually significant flexibility about the amount of downpayment and the number of years over which the remaining mortgage balance will be amortized. There are also choices regarding the structure of the mortgage—whether it is a fixed rate for the period of the mortgage or a flexible rate which is adjusted periodically based on interest rates in the marketplace. As we have said before, there is no one way which is right for everyone. The considerations include availability of cash, willingness to tie up cash in a primary residence, comfort with debt, cash flow or monthly payments, and tolerance for fluctuations in the future.

It is a good idea for Elizabeth also to call upon someone with legal expertise, who has knowledge of the real estate field, to review the final contract. While this is not a protracted or difficult step, Elizabeth needs to make certain that she understands and is comfortable with the legal document she is signing.

After using her advisors to assist her in the decision-making process, and after shopping her alternatives and making a decision, there is only one person who can take the next important step to implement the decision itself. It is Elizabeth who will have to sign her name to the contract and write a check to complete the transaction. That makes the final decision, Elizabeth's decision and the final action, Elizabeth's action. That's why it is so important for her to be comfortable making that decision and taking that action.

While caution in decision-making and action-taking is simply being realistic and judicious, Elizabeth can also look at the entire process as an exciting adventure which is not only fun, but also a growing experience for her in many ways. That's an attitude of mind which only Elizabeth can control. Even before deciding on whether to buy a condominium, an earlier decision might well be to see the experience of home-hunting as an enjoyable quest. It is more likely then that it will be a successful experience.

Providing For Older Parents

One of the decisions facing many people today relates to the support of older parents. Because of the tremendously high inflationary period we experienced in the '70s and early '80s, many retired people who had felt comfortable suddenly discovered that the comfort rug had been snatched out from under them. Obviously, they have decisions to make, such as seriously cutting back in their expenditures, finding ways of making extra money, or repositioning assets to create more income to continue to do the things they enjoy. While Social Security has increased slightly over the last 10 to 15 years, it has in no way kept pace with the impact of inflation. Today, there are many families in which the older parents are not as financially independent as they thought they might be, and, of course, there are situations in which either poor health or other unexpected occurrences have created dependence.

Let's take a look at Keith and Doris in their mid-40's, who are coping with many financial challenges and demands of their own, including children in college. At the same time, they're concerned about their parents' growing need for additional financial help and they want to allocate some financial resources to assist them in their later years. What are the considerations? Well, here are a few:

1. A primary consideration, obviously, is the attitude and feelings of their parents. It can be humiliating for parents, after a lifetime of pride in taking care of their children, to have the tables turned and ask for help. The way this is handled is critical. While older parents often object quickly to any support whatsoever, I have seen many who did accept assistance from their children or from others when it was provided in a way that allowed them to maintain their dignity. This requires communication between the individuals involved.

2. A careful inventory of the situation is extremely important. Keith and Doris may be able to uncover financial resources which either they or their parents currently own which can be converted into income-producing assets for the parents' benefit.

For example, in a similar case, the parents were strongly committed emotionally to maintaining their home and passing it on to their children after their deaths. The home was quite expensive, and the mortgage was paid off. Since the children were ultimately going to receive the home anyway, they established an arrangement through which they could begin to purchase the home today and pay for it over the rest of their parents' lifetimes.

They actually entered into what is called a private annuity, using the life expectancy tables for annuities, and were able to pay their parents a monthly amount prescribed by the annuity contract in exchange for the ownership of the home. Another possibility might have been an installment sale arrangement. Both legal and tax advisors can assist in exploring alternatives which are appropriate for the people involved.

107

In another case, the energy and creativity of the older parents were such that they were prime candidates for turning a hobby of theirs into a money-making business. What they lacked was initial capital and the business management to make it work. In this case, the children, who were middle-aged, set up their parents in a business which was both personally and financially rewarding for them.

In situations where poor health or other circumstances call for extensive care and where the creative alternatives may be limited, the more direct methods of support may be necessary. Suppose Keith and Doris are forced to use part of their income to supplement the income of their parents. They must decide between taking part of their passive income from investments or using their regular income from salary. In this case, it will be important for them to meet with a tax or financial advisor and determine the most advantageous arrangement based on their specific financial circumstances.

In a similar case, for example, without much thought or planning, a middle-age couple in a fairly high-tax bracket took one of their tax-free municipal bonds and placed it in a trust for their parents. The tax bracket of the older parents was very low, comparatively speaking. This meant that the benefit of the tax-free bond was greatly reduced. It would have probably been better had they used another asset to fund the trust and kept the tax-free bond income for themselves.

In planning for the support of older parents, decision-making must take into account people's feelings, the financial facts, and other factors involved in careful planning.

Similar considerations have to be taken into account in planning for handicapped children or other disadvantaged adult family members.

Decisions In A Divorce

Another significant trend of the times which calls for extensive and varied decisions is the growing incidence of divorce. Statistics tell us that more than half of the marriages end in divorce. That means that more than half of the couples who get married and put their financial resources together have to go through the process of untangling financially. I have no suggestions on how to make divorce easy. It does create the necessity, however, of decisions and actions which, if they're based on a thoughtful planning process rather than on emotional reaction, can benefit everyone concerned.

Some factors to consider in the divorce situation are:

1. The separate or individual resources of each party. What does each individual already own in his or her name and what is their separate potential for earning income?

2. What assets do they jointly own which they would be willing to sell, and which assets do they desire to divide or transfer from one to the other?

3. Which assets require either management attention or expertise which might be possessed by one of the marriage partners and not by the other?

4. How can they help each other make that financial transition in the short- and long-term?

5. When there is bitterness and resentment and an emotional reaction to the divorce process, some tragedies occur which could be avoided. For example, it is not uncommon for one divorced spouse to end up with a home but with no visible means of support for maintaining it—and later resent the fact that the home had to be sold. The fight over the house was so emotional that financial realities were overlooked.

6. The tax situation of each marriage partner in the new divorced situation should be taken into consideration in the decisions which are made, with special consideration of the laws affecting child support and alimony.

109

Since some divorces are more friendly than others, and since children may or may not be involved, circumstances vary greatly from one situation to another. However, since money is an expression of what we really want out of life, when two people have decided they want to live their lives separately, every effort they can make to decide carefully how to put money in place to accomplish their objectives is time well spent.

Starting A New Business

One of the dreams of a great many people seems to be to start their own business. Yet, statistics tell us that more than half of new small businesses fail. Therefore, whether you are thinking about starting a small business as a supplement to a full-time job and having someone else manage it for you, or whether you are thinking about a business in which you will be involved full time (that may mean 16 to 18 hours per day), it might be well to look at some of the considerations important in the decision-making and implementation process related to starting a small business. Here are a few:

1. How much money will it take to get the business started? What is the additional capital required for the purchase of materials, supplies, equipment, etc.?

2. What will be the monthly operating cost of the business including wages, salaries, payroll taxes, benefits, utilities, rent, telephone, legal and accounting fees, etc.?

3. What is a realistic projection of a break-even point for the business in terms of both dollars and time?

4. What resources do you have financially to be able to continue to operate the business until it is profitable?

5. What are the legal ramifications of being in the particular business you had in mind? Are there licenses or other

requirements, and how long does it take to secure these?

6. How will you measure your success in the business? What benchmark will you use to determine that you are either going to stay with it or get out of the business?

7. What options are there for getting out of the business? Would you have to liquidate, or could you sell or transfer to someone else?

8. What is the competition and the market potential? It would be an excellent idea to spend some time with other people in a similar business listening to their experience, both positive and negative.

9. What are your real reasons for wanting to be in the business, and does the desire to start the business reflect strongly your personal life values?

When you decide to go ahead—which is the big decision—there will then be many small decisions to make to implement that major decision to be a business owner. There will be papers and documents to sign, checks to write, and agreements to be made with all of the various parties who are affected by your decision. We cannot overly emphasize the importance of seeking good competent financial advice including legal, accounting, insurance, and basic business management.

To implement any of your decisions, it will have to be your action which puts everything in place. With competent and caring counsel, you will make a much better decision. However, remember that it is your decision; even if you decide not to decide, that's your decision as well.

ACT-I-ON

I will set a definite date for making a decision in one of the areas of my life in which I have the greatest difficulty deciding what to do.

Douglas is a skilled inventor who has started his own lab to develop innovative new electrical products. He realizes that while he is a risk-taker in experimenting with new scientific techniques, he would hate to risk his money on questionable investments. He needs it too much to provide the equipment he needs for his lab. Yet, since future capital is important for him to continue his work, he wants to invest in something he can count on to assure quick earnings. He doesn't know where to put his money.

CHAPTER 8

Risk/Reward Alternatives

Asking The Right Questions

Think about it. Aren't the most frequently asked questions ones which are general and vague? For example, Richard will ask "Where is a good place to put money?" That really isn't a question for which there is a meaningful answer. Allow me to rephrase the question. "Where is a good place for Richard to put a specific amount of money which he is interested in investing today, based on the results he expects it to produce, the risk he is willing to take to get those results, the amount of time he is willing to let the money work for him, his own personal tax situation, and the purpose he has in mind for the ultimate use of the funds when this specific investment is terminated?"

In fact, if you ask experts, "Where is a good place to put money?", they most certainly will not agree. The opinions of experts are influenced by their own view of economic, political and other factors, as well as personal experience. More importantly, no expert can know what Richard wants from the use of his money until Richard makes it clear.

There is, however, a personal, specific, and practical set of questions which will enable you to know where to invest a certain sum of money at any particular time. To determine that, you must understand yourself as well as you understand the world of investment alternatives. Some of the questions you should consider are:

1. How much money is involved?

2. How long are you willing to leave the investment intact?

3. What expectations do you have regarding the investment performance?

4. Which benefits are most important to you?
   a. safety of principal
   b. current income
   c. appreciation
   d. tax benefits

A fuller discussion of these benefits follows, but remember: no investment can fulfill your expectations if you anticipate 100% in all four of these benefit areas. So we have to select those benefits which are most important to us. In other words, we have to learn to say "no" to that which is unimportant, or of lesser importance, in order to say "yes" to the benefits which matter most.

In the investment world, most people tell us that whatever they own today, in terms of investments, is usually a result of what they have been sold. Someone has convinced them that this was an important place to put money. Most people also tell us that their investment portfolio is somewhat of a hodge-podge. They are not sure it makes a lot of sense and whether it reflects what's really important in terms of their own investment goals. A great many people tell us that they aren't even sure they know what they want in terms of investments. Sometimes people will say, "Well, I just want my investments to make a lot of money. I don't want to take any risks. And I don't like paying taxes." Unfortunately, in the investment world, the real world, it doesn't work that way.

As with every other aspect of living, there are trade-offs. What we must do to get our plan to work for us is to develop our own investment profile. To see how your personal preferences regarding investments can influence your decisions in the investment marketplace, you might consider trying this simple exercise which you can do easily at home.

Investment Profile

Investment Expectations

Safety	0	1	2	3	4	5
Income	0	1	2	3	4	5
Appreciation	0	1	2	3	4	5
Tax Advantages	0	1	2	3	4	5

Investment Profile

Let's take a look at the first part of the investment profile. It's what we call investment expectations. On this chart there are the four benefits we considered earlier: safety, income, appreciation and tax advantages.

Safety means you aren't likely to lose any of your principal investment.

Income means the investment is producing current cash flow.

Appreciation refers to the growth or increase in the basic value of the investment.

Tax Advantages may come in various ways to reduce your overall tax burden.

You might say, "Well, it would be wonderful to have the maximum in all four categories." But as I indicated, investments just don't come that way. That would be batting 1,000, and I don't know anyone who bats 1,000.

So, what you do at the very beginning is to say to yourself, "I'll be a superstar if I bat 500. Out of the total potential of 20 points on this investment expectation chart, if I can select 10 and put these 10 points in the categories which are most important to me, I will have a good running headstart in developing my investment strategy."

It puts you in the right ballpark, and it enables you to feel that you are playing the investment game to be a winner, because your expectations are realistic and you have understood the necessity of the trade-offs.

Investment Profile

Investment Characteristics

	Lo		Med		Hi
Liquidity	☐	☐	☐	☐	☐
Debt	☐	☐	☐	☐	☐
Risk/Return	☐	☐	☐	☐	☐
Management Effort	☐	☐	☐	☐	☐

Now let's look at this second part of the profile. It's what we call investment characteristics.

Here we haven't used quite the same format, but we do have a low, medium, and a high rating for characteristics such as liquidity, debt, risk/return and management effort.

Let's talk about those briefly.

Liquidity is simply cash or the ability to convert to cash very quickly. It is important to ask yourself, for example, "How important is liquidity in my situation?" In other words, how important is it for you to either be in a cash position or be able to quickly convert your investment to cash when necessary?

Debt is obvious. It is either a mortgage or a loan of some kind that has been placed against a property or asset. It's up to you to determine honestly how you feel about debt. To what extent are you willing to be personally obligated to repay debt which is created in association with an investment?

Risk/Return: We do not automatically get a higher return simply because we take a higher risk. But there certainly should be, in any investment that we make, the potential of a greater return if we take a greater risk. The rule of thumb is that, in general, with a lower risk we expect a lower return; with a higher risk we expect a higher return. The question here is, do you want the risk return to be on the low end of the scale, the medium or the high end of the scale.

Finally, look at the "management effort" line on the chart. How involved do you really want to get in an investment? Do you want, very passively, to write a check and have someone else worry about it? Or do you want to actually be involved in decision-making that is related to the management of the investment?

How Do You Really Feel About Risk?

To discuss the matter of risk/reward further, an important question is, "To what degree am I willing to experience uncertainty in anticipation of a greater return?"

In other words, is what you "want" compatible with your emotional response to risk?

If you invest in something which keeps you awake at night, frightens you to death, or is a project which you do not even believe in, simply because of the promise of making some money, it is unlikely that it will turn out to be the right investment for you. Even passive investments, investments which you do not manage or control, need to be ones with which you are comfortable.

Everything may not go as we plan. There are risks which could virtually destroy our enjoyment of the present and potential for the future.

There are some risks where the stakes are too high. There are gambles not worth taking. On the other hand, little risk usually means little reward.

The critical question is whether you can accept and recover from a decision which didn't work out the way you planned. One of the inside-out planning questions which should be asked before you take any risk in the investment area is as follows:

"Would it disturb you more to lose an opportunity for significant gain or to experience a significant loss?"

If you can answer that question honestly, you have given yourself investment direction.

There are risks, of course, which should not be taken, because there would be no way to recover from them. These fall not only in the area of investing, but also in the category we usually define as risk management. The basic guideline is: "Retain the risk you can afford and transfer (insure) the risk you cannot afford."

Examples:

1. The risk of losing your income if you do not have sufficient assets to provide income during a period of disability. The obvious solution to this problem is transferring that risk through insurance to protect against the loss of income due to sickness or accident.

2. Risks related to health which can involve extensive medical and hospital costs. Those are risks medical insurance is designed to help us manage, and in this area it is the major medical expenses which are the main concern.

3. The event of death in a situation where the deceased was a significant provider of income to others who were dependent upon him or her. There is no way to solve this problem other than through adequate life insurance to create assets to provide income to the survivors.

4. The risk associated with a personal liability suit. It is very unlikely that you will be sued for personal liability in any significant amount; however, that event would only need to occur once to play havoc with all of your other financial planning. The low cost of insuring that risk suggests strongly that you not gamble in that regard.

5. Risks associated with the loss of property due to theft, fire or other causes. That's where property and casualty insurance comes in.

Investing In Real Estate

Once in a while, people say, "I'd recommend you invest in real estate; not too much risk in that." The truth is, they have told you nothing of significance.

Real estate, as a matter of fact, can range all the way from undeveloped raw land in a highly speculative location to a fully-leased income-producing office building with leasing contracts which escalate each year and which are being paid or fulfilled by financially solid leasing tenants.

You can purchase real estate on a cash basis, or leverage with as little down as possible and a mortgage that is as large as you can afford.

You can buy investment property directly and get involved in the management responsibilities, or you can invest in real estate through limited partnerships. The risk is different in each case.

In all of these situations, the real estate itself, the structure of the purchase and the responsibilities for management make each investment dramatically different. In fact, there is more similarity sometimes in investments in totally different product areas with similar investment structures than there is in investment of identical products with dissimilar investment structures.

Real estate, or any other investment vehicle, therefore, may be relatively risk-free or risk-laden.

It is wise to learn as much as you can about the risk characteristics of any investment you are considering and wiser to match it, as you plan from the inside-out, to your own personal risk-tolerance.

Let me take the category of "management effort" as another example of how the chart really works. If I indicated on this profile that I had a very low desire to get involved in the management effort of my investment, I would certainly not want to go out and buy single family houses, duplexes, quadraplexes, or other kinds of rental property and have to fix them up, rent them out, keep them rented and manage them. That's not the right investment for me.

I may want to be in real estate, but I would want to be in limited partnerships or the investments in the real estate world where someone else is doing the managing and where I am simply taking a more passive role.

Let's take the stock market as another example. If I am high in my management effort scale, I may want to actually be much more involved in investing in the market, making decisions to buy and sell stocks. If, however, I want to be in the stock market but I am low on the management scale, a managed mutual fund is certainly far more appropriate for me to accomplish my objectives. If I have sufficient funds, I may even be able to benefit from a professional portfolio manager.

Investment Priorities

Establishing your investment priorities can be most useful. Instead of relying on the myriad of financial ads you read or on opportunities which salespeople bring to you, you can go confidently to an advisor in the marketplace with your own criteria and together select those investments which fit your needs.

We've known people who approached someone and asked the commonplace general question we referred to earlier: "Where's a good place to put money?" All too often, with no more input than that, they got an answer. Then they went back home and completed this exercise. When they returned to the same advisory source, they said, "I would like to know a good place to put my money—but first, I want to show you something that will help us discuss what's going to work best for me."

The result this time was totally different in terms of output from the advisor because there was now some meaningful input from the client.

I highly recommend that you take this exercise seriously and use it. It can make a difference, a significant difference in getting what you want from your life and your money.

ACT-I-ON

1. I will complete my own charts of Investment Expectations and Investment Characteristics.

2. I will compare my current investments to my charts.

3. I will discuss the results with an investment advisor to determine how I might correct any inconsistencies.

Cindy and Rick decided six years ago, when their first child was born, to write their wills. Why, then, six years later, do they still have no wills?

Bert, at age 46, is a confirmed bachelor. He has some money he wants to invest, which is a combination of an inheritance and money he has saved and accumulated over the years. It's just sitting in a traditional checking account, and he feels the need to put the money to work in a diversified investment portfolio. In fact, he has made the decision several times, over the past few years, to launch a more aggressive investment program. The money, however, is still "running on idle" in his conservative parking lot.

CHAPTER 9

It's More Than Just Deciding

Implementing Decisions

At this point, you have been realistic about what you want and what you have. You have also made some important decisions about what you must do in order to use what you have to get what you want in life.

The next step, obviously, is to take the action required, to actually implement the decisions that you made.

You can use, of course, advisors from many different aspects of the financial field to help you. If you have one primary advisor who is working with you to coordinate the whole process and eliminate overlapping and gaps, chances are you are more likely to actually get the action steps taken. A good advisor will be there to make certain that you follow through and get the job done.

The story is told that a man went to his physician. The X-rays were taken and the result, after careful deliberation, was that surgery was recommended. The patient was hesitant and the doctor somewhat facetiously said, "Well, I guess if you don't want surgery, we could touch up the X-rays." We could make the point that if our financial X-ray indicates that we need to do some surgery on our cash flow situation and our balance sheet or, more importantly, on our actual financial behavior, then touching up the financial X-rays isn't going to make any difference. Your implementation plan needs to correct what's wrong with your current financial picture and keep you financially healthy and strong in the future.

_____

Throughout this book, we've been talking about the need to take action. If you determine that you desire to implement your own plan, it is even more important to list what "ACT-I-ON" steps you will take. Your checklist needs at least two columns:

— *What* needs to be done?

— *When* am I going to get it done?

Act-i-on

WHAT	WHEN
• Get wills done	Next 30 days
• Transfer money to tax-free account	End of this week

If you decide to utilize a primary advisor, the advisor should work with you to develop your checklist. In this case, your checklist needs to include:

— *Who* is responsible for getting it done?

Act-i-on

ACTION ITEM	TARGET DATE FOR COMPLETION	BY WHOM
1. _____	_____	_____
2. _____	_____	_____
3. _____	_____	_____
4. _____	_____	_____
5. _____	_____	_____
6. _____	_____	_____
7. _____	_____	_____
8. _____	_____	_____
9. _____	_____	_____
10. _____	_____	_____

In working with advisors, there will still be some steps that you will have to undertake personally, but much of the implementation can possibly be handled by the advisors, or other financial specialists they recommend.

Implementation Means Follow-Up

If you decided, for example, to save some money, what steps have actually been taken to make sure the savings become real? Maybe you decided to set up a personal savings program. How was the money to get from your personal checking account into some form of personal savings account? Or maybe you were going to sign up for one of the company savings programs and have the funds actually deducted from your check each month or each week. Have you signed the forms that are necessary so that the automatic payroll deduction will take place? What date did you put into the "When" column for taking care of this?

Perhaps you never had a will, (formal, official or legal will) and you have decided that you are going to get it done, or maybe you had one which was drafted a long time ago and you have decided to revise it and make it current. Has that been done? Has the will been signed? My friend Roy said that he was excited because he was finally going to get his will done. I asked Roy what steps he had taken, and he said, "Well, I called my attorney and I told him to get to work on it." Well, obviously the question is, how is Roy's attorney going to work on his will unless he knows what Roy's will is?

A legal document drafted by an attorney is a reflection of your wishes, and you have to communicate those in order to get the process completed. No input to the attorney means no signed documents to complete the project. There are many unsigned wills because people have not set specific target dates or pushed themselves to make sure that the project is completed.

All too often, single people neglect to draw up a will. They care just as much about what will happen to their estate, but there is a tendency to wait. Until they get married. Or until their business or job flourishes and they know more about the size of the estate they might leave. Or until they meet someone whom they might want someday to designate as their beneficiary.

Remember, wills can be changed and so can beneficiaries. The consideration to be kept in mind is that *you* want to be the one who decides what happens to your money. It is your money; it should be controlled by you. Change your will as circumstances dictate, but at least have a legal document to change.

If you recognize the importance of having a will, write it down. Then give yourself a target date to get it done; in the next 30 days, perhaps.

Similar decisions about your insurance program and disability benefits call for a specific listing under *What* and *When* and, if appropriate, *Who*.

You also have to check to see whether the various elements of your plan have been integrated. Sometimes we find that people spend a lot of money to have elaborate trust agreements drafted, and they also secure insurance to fund those trusts. Somehow, however, they never get around to signing the proper documents to make it possible for the insurance to be payable to the trust. So they have this huge vessel which is empty because the insurance is paid in a totally different manner. That is a result of the lack of coordination in planning.

In the area of tax planning, let's assume that you decide to move some of your investment money from one place to another because your decision, after developing a plan, was that you wanted more of your money to be in a tax-free vehicle. When was it done? Are you sure the transaction was completed?

Writing It Down

To start with, a written plan is easier to track than one which is in your mind only. We all have so many old and new thoughts to remember every day. Besides, research tells us that the likelihood of your doing something is geometrically increased when you write it down.

I suspect that some of you have had the experience of going to the grocery store to get only three items, but because you didn't write them down, you couldn't remember one of them when you got to the store. Consider how much more extensive and complex your financial decisions are than grocery items. Write them down!

In listing the *What, When* and *Who* involved in implementing your decisions:

— Make your list pertinent to what is important in your planning.

— Make your list as detailed as possible in order to finish the job.

— Then keep your list handy to remind you of what still has to be done.

For those things that still have to be done, even if you decide to postpone them for the moment, list a target date for reconsidering them and acting on them in the near future.

Remember, only when decisions are implemented can they start working for you.

The American poet John Greenleaf Whittier reminded us that:

"For of all sad words of tongue or pen,
The saddest are these: "It might have been!""

After fully implementing a plan (and that is a major accomplishment for most people), how do you then stay on track? What can you do this year, next year and in the years ahead to make sure that you are continuing to move in the right direction?

It's more than just deciding what you want to do. It's getting it done. If you can do it yourself, great. If you need professional assistance, that could be an investment of time and money which can continue to pay off for years to come.

ACT-I-ON

1. I will review decisions I have made in each of the following areas:

    a. Spending to enjoy today

    b. Saving and investing for the future

    c. Protecting against risks related to my assets, income and survivor needs in the event of my death

    d. Planning related to my taxes.

2. I will determine what my number one decision is and implement that decision by

    _____
    (date)

3. I will assign priorities to any remaining decisions on which I need to act, set target dates, and begin implementing by order of importance to me.

When they were in their late 40's eight years ago, Paul and Grace sat down with a financial advisor. They reviewed and changed their insurance program, updated their wills, projected long-term retirement plans, and set up a college fund for their two children.

When they look at their lives today, however, how dramatically different things are. Only one of the children went to college. Both children are now married, and Paul and Grace have their first grandchild. Paul was recently transferred to his company's home office 1,000 miles away, and Grace is now involved in a new career in the field of interior design.

They remember how thoroughly they planned everything out eight years ago. Their financial plan, however, hasn't been reviewed since then.

CHAPTER 10

A Plan That Keeps On Working

Planning is a lifetime process.

Things can and do change. You need to be able to review your financial situation and respond quickly. Not only do our situations change, but we even change our own minds. When circumstances or our objectives change, we must be able to change our plans as well.

Developing a plan that keeps on working means that we have to continue to:

1. Review the facts

2. Review our own ideas and feelings about the facts.

I cannot overly emphasize either one. Both are critical.

Reviewing Your Plan

Once you are confident that your initial plan has been implemented and really is in force, the next thing to do is to set a date to review it periodically.

How will you know if you are doing well, if you are making progress, unless you have some way of regularly measuring your progress and evaluating the results?

In the plan implementation phase, we emphasized the establishment of expected results and how they will be measured. In other words, there need to be checkpoints to stop and ask, "How are we doing?" There must be, too, an understandable way of measuring results. That's why it is so important to set target dates for the completion of projects, with someone accepting responsibility, someone who is willing to be accountable for following up. In terms of investment results, the only way to gauge progress is to have a method of measurement we understand and trust.

Perhaps you should set a date to review almost every aspect of your planning annually. Changes can occur almost unnoticed unless you go over everything at least once a year.

There also may be reasons why you might want to review your plan, or at least certain aspects of your plan, next quarter or even next month. If so, set some realistic dates for a review in the near future to make sure you are still on track.

Maybe there is an interim date for reviewing because your bonus month will take place seven months from now. That's when you are going to get extra money and you want to determine how best to use those funds before they get lost in the shuffle.

You may set a special date for reviewing, because it's the maturity date for a bond or a certificate of deposit or some other investment vehicle.

Perhaps your key date is the time when you are most likely to be able to pull things together for review.

One word of caution, however: when you set a date, try not to postpone it or change it. We have seen five years go by while people kept putting off their review, waiting for a better time. Set a date— and keep the date.

Effective Monitoring

If monitoring is to be effective, it is important that the expected results be clearly established. Otherwise, it is almost impossible for them to be measured.

Suppose you say, for example, "I'd like to provide a good college education for my children." While that expresses your desires, it gives no indication of how you can reach that goal. Ask yourself, "What does it take to provide a college education for my children? What will the cost of that education be in the future when the children are ready for college?" To plan properly, determine next how much you need to set aside now, or on an annual basis, to assure that funds will be available when that time comes. By being specific, you can measure the results, year by year. Each time we review our progress, we have an opportunity to make changes, if either circumstances have changed, or our goals have.

Let's take another example. With the help of a professional financial advisor, you have determined what is required for financial independence and that it is possible for you to achieve financial independence by age 65 if you start now with new savings of approximately 10 percent of your current and future compensation. You have made assumptions about the rate at which your compensation will increase, and the after-tax rate of return you will receive on your investments. You are committed to this plan of action, and your advisors are aware of the importance of this goal. They, in turn, are committed to help you achieve it. However, unless you are specific in terms of what that means next year and the year after and the year after that, and are able to measure your progress year after year, it will only be a matter of luck if you get there.

Assume you decide to travel across the country in five days. You set out with no plan or checkpoints, and find yourself aimlessly wandering through the countryside and from one city to another—not even sure you are headed in the right direction. It would be best if you didn't have to reach your destination at any certain time, because it will be pure luck if you get there in five days.

To set yourself on a 20-year course without specific checkpoints is to hold no one accountable. In fact, unless your savings are really new savings, and unless you are achieving the after-tax return on investments which you projected, you can be off your course almost before you get started. It is one thing to say, "I had a pretty good year," or "Things are going fairly well." It is another to say, "I actually saved and invested 10 percent of my compensation, and my investment equity increased this year by $10,000 or $20,000," or whatever the facts may be.

The real key to staying on track is good communication. It's keeping the lines of communication open with yourself, with other people in your life and, definitely, with your advisors.

If you change your mind about your goals, for example, but don't communicate verbally with the other people involved, you are likely to make the drastic mistake of assuming they can somehow read your mind. It is extremely helpful to call "time-out" occasionally, go into a huddle with the other players on your team, check signals and decide if your game plan strategy is working.

If it is, you can get back to the game with enthusiasm. If it can be improved, you need to make the changes required and commit to your new game plan.

Coping With Change

Reviewing your plan is especially important in today's fast-paced world, since things can change unexpectedly and often. Life does at times throw us a curve. There are surprises. Even our values may change, and we need to be able to respond quickly to stay on track.

Let's look at a few areas of relatively frequent changes in our society.

—Suppose there are changes in the family situation. Last year you had a great plan but were single, and you just got married. Or last year you were married and your plan made sense, but this year you are divorced or widowed.

—Last year you had children in college, but they're not in college any longer. They graduated or quit. Or last year your children weren't planning to go to college and have now changed their minds. They have begun making plans to go and are asking for your help.

138

—You have older parents. You thought they were okay financially but you've noticed recently that they are cutting back on things. You suspect that it is because their funds may be somewhat tight and they are afraid to spend. You would like to help; you're not really sure how.

—You've moved from one house to another, from one state to another or from one job to another. Changes in your personal or family situation definitely require a change in plans.

—You may also change the way you feel about things. For example, when you did your planning initially, you thought you wanted to keep that second home or place at the lake, but now you aren't so sure. Your children are living in another state, you never use it, you wonder if you really want to hang onto it. Or perhaps you said "no" to a second home when you did your planning, but now, you'd like to explore that possibility. The only way you can approach the planning process and stay on track is, obviously, to stay in touch not only with how you once felt, but with how you feel now.

—Then there also may be changes in circumstances, that are virtually beyond your control, and yet they affect your plans directly.

In the *economic environment*, for example, changes can be rather dramatic. Interest rates were extremely high when Carl did his planning, and now they seem to be moderate or even low, comparatively speaking. On the other hand, Sandra did her planning when interest rates were relatively low and now they are climbing steadily.

There are surprises in the rise and fall of whole industries. You may be investing in one industry which offered considerable promise. If you're into long-term investing, that's one thing, but if you have invested for the short term, you may want to reconsider your strategy. Changes in industries such as transportation or high technology or energy or real estate can surprise even the experts at times, and it could mean that when those surprises or changes occur, you definitely want to review and make some changes in your plans.

Some changes which call for plan revisions may happen just when you think everything is going great. You're feeling good because you finally painstakingly developed a sound plan and implemented it carefully. Then along comes a major change of some kind that seems to knock a hole in everything you have done.

Ralph and Molly, for example, have been successfully operating their family business for over 20 years. They have even set up a plan with their oldest son for the continuation of their business. Recently, they have heard rumors of a new technical development which could make their manufacturing process obsolete.

In reality, the situation may not be as bad as it seems (of course, it could be worse than it seems also). You won't know unless you take time to review. That usually means reviewing in at least two ways: one, review the facts, and two, review your own ideas and feelings about the facts. They are equally important. Both are critical! If you don't have the facts, it's extremely difficult to make an intelligent decision. Since most experts believe that people respond to feelings more than they do to facts, however, you need to clarify what you feel and why.

Staying On Track

There is often a major pitfall somewhere along the planning process for many people. It's so easy to develop a sense of disappointment—which leads to a sense of failure—which can definitely get in the way of their commitment to the ongoing planning process. There are going to be some decisions which don't turn out (in retrospect) to be the best.

Some who experience a setback or disappointment immediately start to look for an excuse for failing. That's usually easy to find. Others, however (and those are the fortunate ones), look for a way to overcome their disappointment and succeed next time.

In fact, in the game of life, most of us are going to make some "bad shots." The key is to keep our last bad shot in perspective. Even when you watch professional athletes play an almost perfect game, you always see them make some bad shots. What makes them professional is that they are ready to make changes in their game in order to correct and improve. Instead of lamenting the past, they focus on what they need to do to succeed in the future.

Planning: A Lifetime Process

On a personal note, I definitely want to live, I mean really live, until the day I die. Even if one day I retire from the formal business of working, I don't ever want to retire from the business of living.

I know that I want to continue being involved in things I enjoy and to experience life as completely as possible as long as I live.

So my commitment today is to make a plan that looks as if it's going to work for me, and I will continue to review and change it as often as I have to so that it will continue to be my plan and work for me—as long as I live.

I encourage you to make a similar commitment—to your own plan. One that will work for you as long as you live.

In a radio address on his ninetieth birthday, Justice Oliver Wendell Holmes pointed out: "The riders in a race do not stop short when they reach the goal. There is a little finishing canter before coming to a standstill . . . For to live is to function. That is all there is in living."

If to live is to function, your financial plan must allow you to function well, with peace of mind, knowing that your money has indeed been put in place to make possible all the things that have been of greatest importance to you throughout the years. That requires you to balance the enjoyment of today with the security of tomorrow—and to make inside-out planning a lifetime process.

ACT-I-ON

1. I will set a date for the review of my progress against my total financial plan.

2. I will identify any changes in attitude, situation or results desired.

3. I will revise my plan accordingly.

Since he started a business of his own, Phil has seen it grow steadily. Today, it is the largest travel agency in his city. Together, he and Helen, his wife who assists him in the agency, have created a sizable savings account.

The questions they keep asking are: What to do with the money? Where should they invest? Whom should they trust to advise them? How much risk are they willing to take?

At this point, Helen would like to open a gift shop of her own, but isn't sure she would succeed without Phil's help. There are other things she might enjoy too.

There are many confusing alternatives—for their personal goals and for the investments they should make. They read a lot. They discuss their ideas, but do nothing. How can they overcome what seems to be a "paralysis of analysis?"

CHAPTER 11

Choosing And Using Advisors

Who Needs An Advisor?

Obviously, Phil and Helen (on the preceding page) need some professional advice on how to get started. Other people may recognize a need for counseling at different points in their lives.

Consider the following scenarios which are fairly typical of the experiences of other people who then turned to a professional financial advisor. The first step, in each case, was an awareness of the realities in their own situation.

Scenario #1. Several years ago, Chuck started his own health foods store which, after two difficult years, has now become a successful business. Yet Chuck is not experiencing either the personal satisfaction or the financial security which he was certain would come with increased earnings. Also, because his business was slow in getting started, he's not sure for how long he can maintain its success or whether he will ever become financially independent in the future.

Chuck is quite aware that the management of his financial affairs is important, but after putting in long hours in his store, the last thing Chuck wants to do is to spend his evenings dealing with his own personal financial affairs—much less explore alternatives related to investments, tax planning or insurance programs.

Besides, Chuck is not at all sure to whom he should turn for assistance. Is it a financial planner, an attorney, a tax specialist, insurance expert, investment counselor, or some other specialist who would be most appropriate in his situation?

Scenario #2. Although Al is now a supervisor at a large printing company, making money has never been easy. Somehow the salary increases are barely sufficient to keep him afloat, and bonuses are few and far between. The money is usually spent before Al gets it, since he always seems to be borrowing to maintain his interest in new technology, which includes a computer system, new software programs as they become available, a new stereo system, VCR's and compact disk player.

His credit, of course, is excellent. That's what all of the money-lenders keep telling him when they extend credit for him to consolidate bills or purchase those items he wants but cannot afford. Al keeps waiting for that big job opportunity, raise or bonus which will clearly put him in the black. However, each new day the challenge is simply to make ends meet. There is always more month remaining at the end of the money. When will the day come when he has some money remaining at the end of the month?

Al also worries about the future when he will no longer be able to earn enough to support himself. Looking back, Al is making a lot more money today than he did ten years ago. However, it doesn't appear that he is any better off than he was many years ago. He would love to learn how to manage his money, if only he had some money to manage.

Scenario #3. During Wayne's lifetime there have been many peaks and valleys. There were times when he had considerable money in the bank, his investments went well, and he was able to demonstrate a significant "net worth" on paper.

Wayne is an entrepreneur, starting and selling businesses and going in and out of the stock market. Many of his ventures have been successful and, for a while, becoming a millionaire was not just a dream, it became a reality. In between the successes, however, were the losses. Win or lose, Wayne kept going to the table with all of his resources whenever he found an opportunity which was significant enough to take the big chance.

Although he realizes that erratic income may have been largely responsible for his first two marriages ending in divorce, Wayne continues to "hang in there."

He's now planning to marry again and, at this point, Wayne is beginning to wonder whether he may find himself one day at the end of the road with very little to show for all of his risk-taking ability. The dramatic contrast between having money to burn one day and searching frantically for money to borrow the next day is no longer exciting.

Although he has said to himself many times, "I need to learn to manage the money I make," there is the growing awareness that he needs to take a hard look at his "all or nothing" approach to business. Wayne is beginning to wonder if he might need some counseling on the management of his life as well as the management of his money.

Scenario #4. Suzanne has a very good job as a fashion consultant and is making more money than she ever dreamed possible. She recognizes that her career potential is excellent, but most of the time she feels uncertain about the future. She feels that no matter how much money she may accumulate, it may not be enough because of all the problems associated with taxes and inflation, problems which she continues to fear although she does not really understand them.

Suzanne assumes that she'll get married someday and her financial picture may change. But in the meantime, she puts most of what she earns directly into a bank account. Although she would like to visit her sister on the West Coast, and would like a larger apartment, she feels she should save her money instead. Needless to say,

Suzanne is not fully enjoying her life. Because of her obsessive need to prepare for the future, she is denying herself many pleasures today.

Scenario #5. Stan knows that he works for an excellent company. He likes his job, enjoys his relationship with other employees, and shares the enthusiasm of the company for its future growth potential. In fact, he feels that he can make a significant contribution to the progress of the company. When he stops occasionally to consider the benefits offered by the company, he is appreciative. There is, however, a vague sort of gap between his understanding of the benefits and genuine appreciation for what they mean to him. Take the pension plan, for example. Just last week he received a computer printout of the projected pension benefits at age 65. Just before he stuffed the printout in his desk drawer, he remembered thinking, "I wonder what the benefit will really be since my income is obviously going to increase between now and then. In 20 years, with the effects of inflation on my cost of living, the benefits don't look all that great."

Then there is the life insurance program provided by the company. It's nice, but Stan isn't sure whether it's adequate for his needs. An insurance agent has been encouraging him to obtain an additional policy and, frankly, Stan doesn't know whether he needs it or not. What Stan needs is assistance in analyzing his insurance needs.

For the last month, the company has been announcing and explaining its new incentive savings program with matching funds from the company on part of the employee contribution. It sounds good, but so far, Stan has done nothing. Technically, he understands the way the plan works, but doesn't really know how to evaluate the merits for himself. Would it be better to participate in the plan, or is there some other investment opportunity which might be better? How to evaluate investment alternatives is an awesome challenge for Stan, although he is extremely competent in his executive and management role for the company.

Reaching Out

In all these examples, there was a clear need for professional assistance. Yet they all had concerns such as:

- Whom to trust

- How to open up and share personal information

- How to deal with their own tendency toward procrastination.

They had to recognize that a trusted advisor was a valuable resource and, although an advisor would not change things magically, they could count on his or her commitment to confidentiality, caring and practical assistance.

Selecting Advisors

The role of financial advisor has been described, at various times, as that of educator, coach, catalyst, listener, quarterback and financial expert. Perhaps the best definition of the advisor's role, however, is that of interpreter.

In your own situation, let's say you have decided that your life will not be left to chance, that the way you use your money will reflect your basic personal life values. You are now definitely committed to the planning process.

You also recognize this is something you cannot do all alone. Even if you decide to orchestrate the planning process, there are still other people involved. From time to time you have to call on specialists, experts or professionals to help you make or implement a particular decision. How do you select the attorney, accountant, banker, insurance representative, investment broker, and others when you need to involve them? And — how do you communicate with them to get the results you desire?

Later on we will take a closer look at the role of the primary trusted advisor who coordinates the entire planning process—a role which is becoming increasingly valuable for many people. However, let's examine first the general criteria for selecting all advisors, including a primary financial advisor. What do you need to look for in choosing someone to help you with any of the specific planning areas where expertise is required?

Here are a few basic guidelines:

1. Determine for yourself that the advisor has knowledge and experience in the specialty area. There are, in most professions, certain credentials which are recognized as standard requirements. Find out what those credentials are, and inquire about the potential advisor's background, education and practical experience. In some cases, the individual definitely needs to be affiliated in some way with a larger firm or be able to utilize the resources of other specialists in order to provide professional service.

   Continual education is essential in every profession today. No one can master a professional field once and for all. Ask, therefore, what the advisor has done in the past and is doing currently to keep up in his or her particular area of expertise.

   To locate a financial advisor in your geographical area, you may want to contact one of the following organizations:

Financial Planning Organization (FPA)

5775 Glenridge Drive, Suite B 300 Atlanta, Georgia 30328
(800) 282 PLAN (7526) • www. fpanet.org

The FPA is a membership organization for the financial planning community on a nationwide basis. Its 30,000 members share a common belief that financial planning helps people achieve their goals and dreams.

Certified Financial Planner Board of Standards

1700 Broadway • Suite 2100 • Denver, CO 80290
(888) CFPMARK • (303) 830-7500 • www.cfp-board.org

The CFP Board of Standards grants the right to use the CFP designation to individuals who embrace a code of ethics and rules of governance. It is a regulatory body that administers examinations to candidates, and it owns and has the power to revoke the CFP designation.

National Association of Personal Financial Advisors (NAPFA)

355 West Dundee Rd, Suite 200 • Buffalo Grove, IL 60089
(888) FEE-ONLY • (800) 366-2732 • www.napfa.org

This organization provides consumers with a list of financial advisors who offer comprehensive financial planning for a fee. Fee-only planners do not receive commissions for the sale of any product.

These organizations can give you valuable information about the educational backgrounds, special training and years of experience of their member advisors. Upon request, you can even find out how the advisor is compensated for his or her services. If you don't already have an advisor in mind, you can also receive a list of the people in your geographical area who have met their professional qualifications. Once you meet personally with an advisor, it is important, of course, to also discuss the matters of background and experience directly.

2. Inquire about the advisor's reputation and perhaps ask for references among existing clients. Keep in mind that no one is perfect, and be cautious where the reports are too "glowing." It may be a positive sign when there are a few negatives in the picture. However, you certainly want to start out with an advisor who is highly regarded by the clients being served. Rushing into a relationship without taking time to do some reputation checking can be very costly. It may be well not only to check with existing clients, but with other professionals with whom the advisor has been associated in the course of serving clients.

3. Apply the "listening" test very early in your first personal interview. Share what you consider to be your most important basic life values, and see if the advisor is listening. Does the advisor seem genuinely interested in you and in your life as well as your money? Do you feel the advisor is actively listening and seeking to know you before offering advice on what you should do? Listening is an extremely important aspect of communicating and communication is a two-way street. You are more likely to listen to advisors who have demonstrated their willingness to listen to you. If the advice comes too

early, it is probably too arbitrary or too "canned." It was not designed with you in mind. For the relationship to be effective on a long-term basis, you need a listening advisor.

4. Find out how the advisor works with other professionals to formulate and implement your plan. When you find an advisor who insists on working alone without communicating with other professionals, this is a warning sign. A logical question to ask is "How can one person know everything there is to know about all of the areas which come into play in your total life planning?" In the comprehensive process of getting your financial resources integrated to help you accomplish what you desire in your life, there are areas of specific expertise required. An advisor who is committed to your best interests will welcome ideas from others who are attempting to serve you, and will take initiative to seek out the expertise of other professionals. In both the decision-making and implementation process, your primary advisor will serve as a coordinator.

5. Discuss all compensation arrangements and understand clearly the fees and/or commissions involved. How will the advisor be paid, and how much will the compensation be under various approaches to the planning and implementation process? If the advisor is reluctant to fully disclose this information, you naturally wonder why. In fact, most advisors will volunteer this information very early in order to help you get to know them and how they work. Expect an advisor to explain the fee structure for professional financial transactions. If this information is not provided voluntarily, ask for it. Registered Investment Advisors are required by Security Exchange Commission regulations to disclose compensation arrangements.

There is no fee or commission arrangement which is guaranteed to work best. Paying an advisor less does not

152

mean you got a bargain, and paying more doesn't insure greater value. However, the key is knowing what you are expected to pay and what benefits you can reasonably expect. When all compensation arrangements are fully disclosed, you are able to discuss and evaluate the cost/benefit ratio.

6. Establish the long-term commitment of the advisor to review your plan and assist in making the changes which are advisable. From the beginning there needs to be a game plan strategy for following through, taking action, and periodically checking on your progress to determine what needs to be done to stay on track.

   If an advisor is eager to make a sale and move on, the relationship may be very short-lived and the results totally unsatisfying for you. This guideline is complementary to the third guideline which tests the advisor's desire to "listen" and respond to "you." If the relationship begins that way, it has a better chance of continuing and achieving what is best for everyone.

7. Evaluate the "comfort level" for you and other people involved with the advisor. This is somewhat intangible, yet it is essential for a long-term effective relationship. If you are not comfortable, discuss your discomfort. Raise your questions. Talk about the areas in which you want to see changes take place. If you are simply not able to get comfortable with one particular advisor, it may be advisable to seek out someone else.

   The key in the selection process is defining the assistance required in your situation and determining a mutually agreeable compensation arrangement which will make it possible for you and your advisors to work together effectively.

Sometimes, with the primary advisor in the picture, coordinating the process, the likelihood of getting the various other advisors to work together as a team is greatly increased. That is, of course, if the primary advisor is not only capable, but committed to following through on your behalf.

Communication And Respect

The development of a plan that works involves a real partnership between client and advisor. The key is clear communication and a basic confidence in each other. You need to have respect for your advisor and, likewise, your advisor needs to have respect for you.

In the long run, the measure of your financial plan's success is not whether you have achieved a percent or two greater return on money, saved a few extra dollars in taxes, or even improved in general the performance of your overall portfolio. While all of those are important, the overriding measure of success is how well your plan achieves your personal objectives.

Emily, who has been widowed for 15 years, is someone whose planning illustrates the importance of communication between client and financial advisor, as well as the need for understanding and respecting a client's personal values.

Emily's major asset is a farm which her husband purchased early in their marriage and actively farmed during his lifetime. They borrowed against the farm in lean times and when he expanded his farming operation. At the time of his death, he still had a loan against the farm of about $20,000. It was an old loan with an interest rate of approximately 5 1/2% and a schedule for paying it off which did not require any acceleration of the payment schedule.

When she first met with a financial advisor, Emily had another 10 years in which to pay off the low-interest loan. She had assets invested which were growing at approximately 12% to 14% with which she could pay off the loan, and she was considering doing so because it would enable her to be completely out of debt. Her financial advisor pointed out there would be a financial gain if she continued on the payment schedule for the low-interest loan while leaving her money invested at a much higher rate of return. She had the option at any time of changing her mind and paying off the old farm note, but since her resources were limited, her financial advisor suggested that this approach would enhance her financial security. The two of them discussed various aspects of the situation and both were comfortable with the decision to leave the old farm note in place.

However, a couple of years later, a question now arose as to whether Emily should continue to hold on to the farm or sell it. No longer active in working the farm, she now rents it out to a neighbor, but the income from the rent is barely adequate. In fact, she has started doing some part-time work to supplement her income. Moreover, the market value of the farm seems to be declining. When Emily discusses the new situation with her financial advisor, the following points surface:

1) From a purely financial standpoint, there may be merit in selling the farm today and reinvesting those funds to create a more significant current income and to stabilize the underlying value of her capital base. She could sell most of the farm acreage to her neighbor or another potential buyer, and still maintain her home and a few acres where she could continue to garden and enjoy her lifestyle in the country.

2) From the standpoint of security, Emily indicates that she has confidence in the underlying value of the land on a long-term basis. It has always been there and has taken care of her family for over 40 years. She realizes that times have changed, but she hasn't yet been able to transfer her confidence to other investments.

3) She has a genuine love for the land which makes her want to keep it in the family, whether her children eventually decide to farm the land or not.

155

4) While she is working part-time to supplement her income, she says that she actually enjoys the work. It is personally fulfilling for her. She needs something to do with her time, and it keeps her active and involved with other people. So, she isn't working just for the money.

5) At age 68, her life expectancy is probably another 15 to 20 years. There seems to be no danger of her outliving her capital base unless the value of the farm were to decline drastically or she suddenly started spending much more money every year. Since the farm is situated close to a small city with future potential growth, she will probably be able to sell portions of the farm over the next several years if that becomes necessary or advisable.

Conclusion: Although most economists, from a strictly analytical standpoint, would probably recommend the sale of the farm and re-investment of the assets, the financial advisor listens closely to what Emily is saying about what is important to her. He supports her decision to continue to own the farm, at least for the time being.

Regardless of how one might evaluate the situation logically or from any other point of view, the fact is that from Emily's perspective, the peace of mind Emily feels from holding on to her land is a value that transcends monetary gain.

In an uncertain world where things such as the value of land and other property continues to change, it would be a mistake for either a financial advisor or client to take a short-range view in making important financial decisions. Who knows? In the next 10 years, holding on to that land might have been the smartest thing that could have been done, even from a purely financial standpoint. If anyone could predict that with certainty, they would have found a secret to financial success which doesn't appear to exist.

Being Specific

In every financial plan, there are certain basic ingredients which are essential. You should, for example, have clearly stated your goals and objectives. There should be an analysis of any problems involved as well as observations regarding the unrealized potential in your situation. In the actual establishment of a plan of action, the more specific and detailed the items, the more likely you are to succeed in your planning process.

In other words, it's not just a matter of saying, "I need to purchase more insurance," or "I need a tax shelter," or "I need a will and perhaps a trust." It is a matter of defining the amount of insurance, the type, and perhaps even the potential sources for securing the insurance coverage. It is a matter of spelling out specific investments and dates on which the investments will be made, and it's a matter of putting in writing your estate planning objectives, in order to provide guidance for legal counsel.

As an example, in the estate planning area, you will need to let your legal counsel know to whom you want your assets distributed upon your death and in what proportions. If there are any special bequests for which you have particular plans, you need to itemize these carefully. Where there are special needs involved, educationally, medically, or financially, for either your spouse, children, parents, or others, those need to be outlined in detail.

In the event of your death or your spouse's death, at what ages do you want your children to receive any assets to be distributed to them? Do you want to make bequests to your church, synagogue or other charitable organization? If so, when and in what amounts? Who is to manage the investment of assets upon your death? Someone needs to be named specifically—either an institution or an individual or a combination thereof. What is to happen to your estate if no other person in your immediate family is living, neither spouse nor children? Where do your estate assets go in that event? And, you need, of course, to name a personal representative for your estate as well.

If trusts are involved, the trustees must be chosen, and where minor children are involved, the guardians for those children must be designated. There are other items, but this is an indication of the kind of detail which needs to be spelled out in your planning process. You will receive much better cooperation and achieve more satisfactory results if you have done your homework in preparation for the implementing of your plans.

Be Part Of The Process

Needless to say, professional advisors are essential. We cannot do everything for ourselves. An attorney is needed for legal matters and document-writing such as wills, business structures, partnership agreements, etc. An accountant can be valuable in advising us about tax matters. When purchasing insurance, we need a licensed specialist in the insurance field.

You, yourself, need to be an active participant in the process, however. It's your life and your fate at stake. You stand to gain or lose more than anyone else.

The very first investment you might make is in yourself. Take the time to assess your own strengths and weaknesses, current achievements, and potential needs and desires. What are the personal resources you possess which create opportunities for you today and offer additional excitement for the future?

To invest in yourself, you have to believe in yourself, and make a commitment to the positive possibilities in your own situation.

In many instances, receiving personal, specific, and practical advice is only possible if you are providing your advisors with personal, specific and practical information.

You are familiar with "garbage in garbage out" (GIGO) terminology in the computer field. The same is true in your relationship with advisors.

ACT-I-ON

1. I will secure information regarding professional financial advisors in my geographical area and set a date to interview at least one.

2. I will make a list of concerns to address.

3. I will make a list of questions to ask.

CHAPTER 12

Where Do We Go From Here?

The revolutionary changes that are taking place in the financial services field today seem somewhat overwhelming to many consumers. The growing need for financial planning and sophisticated financial services has brought about an expanding industry.

There are already many large financial conglomerates emerging on the scene and offering services which almost seem identical. There are, at the same time, a growing number of specialized financial boutique shops, offering more personalized services. There will continue to be individual advisors who function in a somewhat independent fashion. Technology, with all of the new services of the computer and other forms of automation, will certainly make our sources of advice and the coordination of that advice a new ballgame. There is, as well, a huge question mark hovering over the role of the government in our financial future. This question mark applies to regulation and deregulation of financial institutions, to perennial changes in the tax laws, to the impact of politics on our general economy, and certainly to the Social Security and other services administered by the government.

Just when you think you are about to understand what's happening, it is not happening anymore. There is a whole new set of rules, a whole new ballgame, and you have to revise your strategy if you expect to succeed. It is not easy in such a confusing set of circumstances to maintain enthusiasm for the planning process. However, the alternative of trying to survive without a plan is even more chaotic.

Fortunately, there is already a strong core of professional advisors, knowledgeable and experienced, who can help you through the planning and review process. As more and more individuals recognize the importance of planning, the need for such advisors will grow rapidly.

Future Planning

It seems to me that the wave of the future in financial planning will have at least three separate and distinct, but complementary, elements.

Wave 1: Education. First, there will be an increasing number of financial education seminars and workshops provided for people in all kinds of groups—corporations, associations, special professional groups and others who come together as a result of a sponsoring institution. Comprehensive and unbiased, they will focus on the involvement of the participants in their own personal growth and awareness-building.

While such seminars and workshops will provide little in terms of technical information regarding the multitude of investment, tax, legal and insurance alternatives, they will enable the participants to begin the financial planning process. Personalized exercises will provide increased understanding to the participants of their own personal values, goals and objectives. They will undoubtedly include value clarification exercises as well as opportunities to use some basic tools such as compound interest tables and calculators. Experiences will be designed to build personal confidence, create trust in the financial planning process, and learn how to utilize professional advisors.

These seminar workshops will present the financial planning process as an exciting lifetime adventure versus a "quick fix."

In-depth seminars and workshops will probably be repeated for participants in many corporations and associations on an annual or bi-annual basis, serving as a review and checkpoint for many people. However, it will be clear that the seminar/workshop is only a place to start. It is not an end in itself.

Wave 2: Advisors. The second wave of the future, I believe, will be an increasing number of highly qualified professional financial advisors who are available to work with clients in an interactive style. Their people skills will be as significant as their technical skills. Many will come from backgrounds in which they were counselors in other professions. There will be a healthy blending of technical and financial expertise and knowledge of human behavior. Most important, professional advisors in the financial field will increasingly be committed to the best interest of their clients.

How we pay for their professional advice is changing, too, with many advisors now charging on a fee basis, rather than receiving only commissions on products sold to implement a plan. We will undoubtedly also see a combination of fees and commissions in the compensation arrangement between advisors and clients. While the source from which the advisor is paid is important, it is not as critical as the understanding between client and advisor about how the advisor is paid, how much he or she is paid, and what that advisory relationship is worth to the client.

Wave 3: Financial Products. The third area in which I see a wave of the future, as deregulation increases, is in the creation of investment, insurance and other financial products and expanded delivery systems for financial products.

While competition in the field among "manufacturers" and wholesalers will create some confusion for a few years, I believe it will bring about a much better end result for everyone concerned. We need the best financial products possible from the clients' perspective and, obviously, they have to be creative and be provided

163

on a profitable basis by those in the product-producing business. It must be a win/win situation or it won't work.

Many of these changes have already started affecting our ability to plan successfully. Access to information and planning resources with the Internet is increasing dramatically.

People today are educated about the importance of money in helping them achieve their personal goals throughout their lives.

There is a growing body of well-trained financial advisors who are dedicated to meeting their clients' individual needs.

There *are* new, updated, wide-ranging financial products for saving or investing geared to people's diverse objectives.

There *are* a vast number of resources available to all of us to make intelligent planning possible. The combination of high tech and high touch makes it possible for us to combine the speed of technology with the very important human element in the planning process.

There is, therefore, no reason to delay planning.

No matter which quarter of your life you are in (and you are neither too young nor too old for this), I encourage you to take "time out" today to check the score, evaluate your game strategy, and develop a specific plan to get ahead.

Only you can start the ball rolling to achieve what you desire.

Only you can determine what is important to you and take steps to bring it about.

Only you know how much money is enough for you to enjoy today and secure tomorrow.

As we've stressed throughout the book, succeeding financially is possible, but it doesn't start with money. It starts with you!